An American Family Sampler

The Founding Generation
1814-1908

Book 1

iBooks
Habent Sua Fata Libelli

iBooks

Manhanset House
Shelter Island Hts., New York 11965-0342
Tel: 212-427-7139
bricktower@aol.com • www.ibooksinc.com

Library of Congress Cataloging-in-Publication Data

An American Family Sampler, The Founding Generation 1814-1908
Mazzella, Donald P. p. cm.

1. History—United States 2. History—Biography
Fiction, I. Title.

978-1-59687-003-1, Hardcover
Book 1

September 2015

First Printing

An American Family Sampler

The Founding Generation 1814-1908

Book 1

CONTENTS

Foreword

Graveyards are temples of solitude and loneliness, yet their inhabitants were once vibrant living beings.

Each grave in a cemetery holds a story. Wander any graveyard and a visitor will find one or two headstones or groupings calling out for further reflection or even research. What did this inscription mean? Why are two women buried on each side of one man's grave but with different surnames? Who was this family with so many interments yet no one remembers them today?

In America toward the end of the nineteenth century, great families, many newly rich or empowered, reserved large places for themselves and their descendants.

By the turn of the twenty-first century, many of these families had petered out or had been absorbed into other clans.

A visitor to Ferndale Cemetery in New Jersey may pass one such enclave whose oldest inhabitant was interred in 1880 and whose newest in 1968. It is the final resting place for a family who for the purposes of this narrative is called Prescott, and who founded and ran a great enterprise through much of America's history.

Just down the path is another group of tombstones for the Gilbert family, beginning in 1899 and ending in 1962.

Some of the oldest visitors might vaguely remember the last name written on most of the first group's tombstones, and other aged visitors might even recognize one name in the second group.

Should that visitor become curious about these inhabitants, there are the newspapers and other archives of their day to peruse.

After diligent efforts, the visitor may know more about these families.

One such visitor did more. The result is chronicled in the book below.

To give the best account of these families—how they lived, how they prospered, and in some cases how they failed—the chronicle is broken down into individual chapters focused on one individual whose tombstone resides here at an important point in that person's life. Through the telling of these key moments, the book is an attempt to weave a mosaic so the reader will know how two families traveled the corridors of time and the American century and ultimately came to rest there in Ferndale.

A note of caution: As any historian will agree, one must look at an individual and his or her actions in the context of that individual's times. Individuals lived their lives and committed deeds based on their experiences and cultural upbringing. It is not our place to judge them by our current standards, but by those of their day. The chronicler has attempted to weave the events surrounding these individuals in order to give the reader a better sense of what informed them. Without this background, one cannot fully appreciate how they lived their lives.

As John O'Hara said, "We all die alone, but it is how we lived that is the story."

The Family Charts

Prescott Family

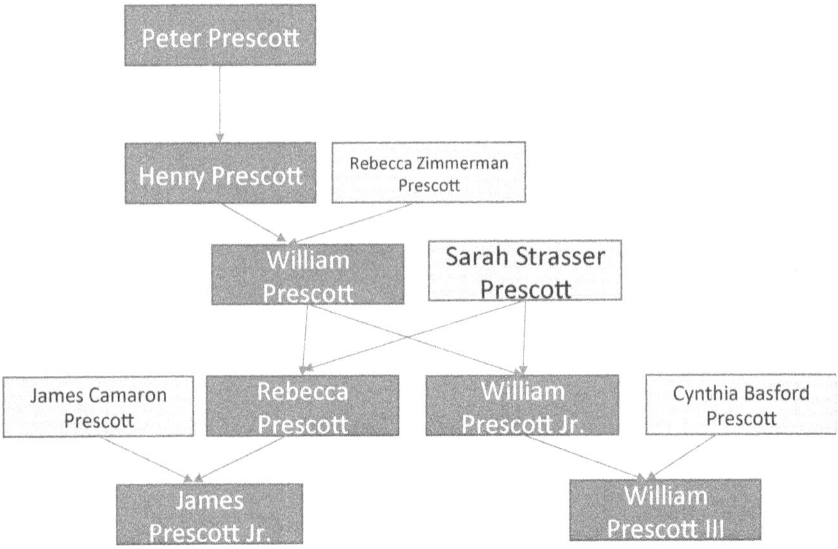
Peter Prescott
Henry Prescott
Rebecca Zimmerman Prescott
William Prescott
Sarah Strasser Prescott
James Camaron Prescott
Rebecca Prescott
William Prescott Jr.
Cynthia Basford Prescott
James Prescott Jr.
William Prescott III

Gilbert Family

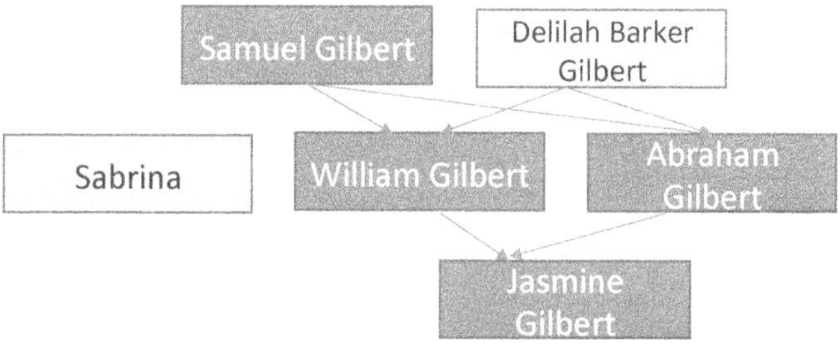

The Founding Generation 1814–1908

Every American family starts with an immigrant. Generally, whatever success and happiness that resulted from this courageous move is found in the story of the succeeding generations.

Members of the first generation came to these shores to seek a better life. They brought old-world ways and skills and applied them to the vast opportunities America offered. In many cases, they also learned to adapt to the New World's methods. The result was a potent blend of innovation and change that built a great empire.

Equally as important, they had an almost fanatical desire to work and succeed. Some succeeded beyond their wildest expectations. Others found heartache, despair, and even death.

Often, whatever happened to the immigrant generation, the next generation found success and even happiness.

One man who succeeded was Peter Prescott. How he did it made him well off but disliked. Like many other immigrants, his son and grandson took what he had done and turned his legacy into a great American business empire.

In many ways, their story is an example of many near generations of other men and women who came to America. What they did, how they did it, and the consequences of their actions on others was—and continues to be—repeated throughout the nation's history. Therefore, it is their lives that this chronicle focuses on.

But because most success stories involve other people, it is important to know why and how these people came within the Prescott orbit.

It is also the story of one family, descendants of those who came to these shores involuntarily—American Blacks.

Peter Prescott 1814

The port official reluctantly stamped the papers on the table in the tiny schooner *North Star*. He smelled something wrong, but the papers said the cargo originated in Charleston, South Carolina.

He had inspected the cargo carefully and even opened a few crates, but they all seemed to be of domestic origin.

"I think there is something about this cargo I don't like, but I cannot find anything amiss, Mr. Prescott."

"I assure you, Mr. Hainesworth, all of these goods came from the South and are of domestic manufacturing."

Both men knew the Embargo and Non-Intercourse Acts were being violated by many merchants like Peter. They had failed to prevent the war with England and had hurt the American economy badly.

Peter had violated both acts almost from their inceptions in 1807 and 1809, and was becoming rich selling contraband goods in the ensuing years.

"The quality is too good," was the terse reply.

"You do not think Americans can produce as good a quality as English craftsmen?"

"Yes, but this furniture and silverware are of as fine a quality as I have seen in a long time. Before the war."

"We have learned much from our English enemies."

"You speak with an English accent."

"But I am an American now. I even voted for our President Madison, God give him strength to pursue this war to its victorious conclusion."

"The British are pressing us hard. They may even be landing on our shores soon in great strength."

"But surely not here in New York."

"Perhaps even our capital."

"Well, may I have my papers and start to unload my cargo?"

"I must say yes though my stomach says you are hiding contraband in those crates and barrels."

"I will be happy to unload and open them all if you like."

"No, I have other duties and you must be on your way."

"Thank you. May I offer you a glass of Madeira from Spain, who is not our enemy?"

Peter took the bottle off a shelf and pulled off the cloth sacking that held it.

"I'll gladly take that. It is cold on these docks."

Peter looked up into the eyes of his captain and got a knowing wink back. He poured the liquid and in a seemingly spontaneous gesture said:

"Please take the rest of the bottle for this cold night."

The port official smiled, stoppered the bottled, and put it in his case along with his copies of the papers.

When he left, Peter turned to the captain, who was making his fifth trip from Charleston to New York for the merchant.

"I'm glad that is over with. I thought for sure he would demand to see every crate and barrel," the captain said.

"It is a cold night and he didn't want to be here through dawn."

"Might he come back and demand we open more cases?"

"I doubt it; I put a gold coin in the sack before giving it to him, and he saw me do it."

The official was not wrong; the goods were contraband from England, the captain rendezvousing at sea off Cape Hatteras with a British cargo ship.

Through his connections in England, Peter was able to obtain and ship goods much wanted by Americans, particularly in the New England states, which were not as supportive of the War of 1812 as other sections of the country.

When unloaded, they would go to the Prescott store or emporium in Connecticut and from there shipped to trusted agents in other Northern states.

It had taken two years to arrange these transactions, and he knew he was breaking many laws by doing so. He didn't care; he was making money at a prodigious rate and building his capital was his only aim.

He had landed in New York thirteen years before almost penniless, and now he had a prosperous business, a pretty wife, and very soon a new baby. He hoped the newborn would be a boy.

"I need an heir to carry out my plans," he thought as he watched the cargo being unloaded.

Peter arrived midmorning the next day to find the doctor in the house.

"You have a new son," the man said curtly. He was Peter's brother-in-law, and like many of the other people in the Orange enclave near Newark, New Jersey, he did not like Peter. His daughter, Penelope, married Peter despite her father's objections.

In the year of their marriage, Peter had done little to endear himself to his wife's family.

Peter cared little for what people thought of him, only that they paid their bills and left him to his business.

As a couple they did not entertain much; Penelope entertained for them when Peter was away on his frequent trips.

Peter rushed to see his son, and when Penelope unveiled him to her husband, he cried out in joy.

It was one of the few times she saw him utter a spontaneous cry.

"We will name him Henry," Peter said, not explaining it was his father's name.

Neither Penelope nor anyone else in America knew much about Peter's origins, and it would remain so his entire life.

Today was one of the highlights of his life: a new son, a shipment that meant his debts were entirely gone—and Prescotts, his company, would have an heir and a clear path to the future.

Henry Prescott 1824

Just ten and somewhat lonely, without the intestinal fortitude he found in his teenage years, Henry Prescott wandered often through the Orange hamlets that dotted the landscape around Newark, New Jersey.

In his time, the waving hills were occupied by little settlements separated by ridges and economic circumstances.

With a curiosity stronger than most boys his age, Henry Prescott escaped his mother's eye to explore the world around him.

One such journey took him to the Negro section of his hamlet, four muddy lanes away from his home.

He wandered through the shacks and lean-tos along the shallow creek bed until he came to a house slightly nicer than the rest.

There a Negro man perched on a beautifully crafted bench was carefully shaping a piece of wood on the rudimentary porch. He stopped to watch as the man shaved the wood, each stroke peeling a thin layer away from the block.

Henry was fascinated by the skill the man displayed. After about ten minutes, the man noticed him.

"You're far from home."

"I'm not, just up the hill."

"Your momma be's looking for you," the man said in a soft Southern drawl.

"Not for a while."

"Well, don't stand gawking at me."

"How'd you learn to do that?"

"My father taught me."

"He sure did a good job."

"If I didn't learn he would have whupped me good."

"My father wants me to learn his business but so far he hasn't whupped me."

"Then you're a lucky boy."

"He don't much talk to me, just lets me look at what he does."

"That's a good way to learn."

"When I'm older, I'll teach him a thing or two."

"That's no way to talk about your pa."

"He'll be glad I did."

"I'm sure he will."

"Did you make that bench you're sitting on?"

"Yes, and just about everything else in our house."

"Your father taught you good."

"I hope so; it's how I make my keep."

"I do a little whittling but nothing like that."

"What do you use to whittle with?"

The boy drew his knife from his trousers and handed it to the man.

George Gilbert took the knife and looked at it gravely.

"Well now, this is a fine knife, from England if I'm not mistaken, and pretty sharp. Have you cut yourself with it while whittling?"

"Once or twice, when I've hit a knot or go too fast trying to lop off some pieces."

"'Well, one thing you got to learn is that whittling takes patience."

"I've got patience, but sometimes the wood doesn't."

"Wood is like everything else in life—it needs patience and the right reason to give itself up to what you want to do."

"Wood's just wood."

"No, that's not true. Each piece of wood is different. You got to learn what it's made of and how best to get to its center."

"Is that what you do?"

"I like to think so."

"How can I learn to whittle right?"

"Well, you can start by sitting next to me and seeing how I do it."

Henry joined the man and sat entranced for an hour as he coaxed a shape from the wood. When he had finished, Henry followed him into the house, where the man fitted it to the top of an unfinished dresser. It almost fit perfectly, needing only one or two flicks from the knife to end up snugly in place.

"That's enough for today, Mr. Henry—your momma be looking for you."

"Why call me Mr. Henry?"

"Old habit. We used to call all white folks at the place where I was born Mr. or Mrs. or Miss."

"Where were you born?

"On Mr. President Washington's estate."

"You mean President Washington? You knew him?"

"As a boy and a man I was one of his people. Now you run along home."

"Can I come back and watch you some more?"

"If your father doesn't object."

"He won't. He says the only thing I need to do is learn everything I can about anything I see or do."

"Now that's a smart man. I'm glad you're listening to your father. My sons won't listen to me. Only Sam my youngest seems to be. He's my youngest, not much older or younger than you."

"I'll be back," shouted Henry as he went off.

He went home and chose another piece of wood to carve. He tried to imitate what the man had done. It was slower, but the results were better.

It was spring when he first visited the Gilbert house, and by summer he had learned much from the man. Sam Gilbert patiently showed him the secrets of his craftsmanship. In an era where white and Negro interaction was not common, the two developed a warm relationship. Because his sons were disinclined to learn his trade, George Gilbert knew he would be the last of his line to be a craftsman.

Henry was fascinated watching the man carve the pieces to the furniture he did for white and Negro customers.

His visits ended when Peter came by and saw him in company with the man.

"Is this where you've been wasting your time?" he said to his son.

"Learning how to craft furniture. You said to learn as much as I could."

"This is no place for you, so git home."

"Mr. Gilbert is a fine craftsman, and we should use him when we need furniture."

"That's why I'm here, but I didn't expect to find you here."

"It's a good trade to have."

"Not for my son."

George Gilbert looked on during the exchange and said nothing.

Henry walked away as his father turned to negotiate with George.

Months later, when the pieces began to arrive in his household, Henry noted one or two pieces he had carved under George's supervision were incorporated into the front of his father's wardrobe.

After his father's death, he had the wardrobe moved to his room, where it remained for the rest of his life.

Two other things he learned from this childhood experience—appreciation of craftsmanship and a better understanding of Negroes.

From the former, he gained an insight that helped him navigate the changes in American life.

From the latter, he was astute enough to find a lifetime helper for his son.

Rebecca Zimmerman 1827

For the first time in her life, Rebecca Zimmerman fully understood the gulf between boys and girls in her community.

Boys were respected, taught, and coddled, but girls were ignored until it came time to marry. The sting of this realization occurred at her younger brother's bar mitzvah when she compared it her own bas mitzvah. In both cases her family and their friends came and joined in the celebration. Her brother Hyman received presents aimed at starting his career in the family business.

Her own gifts were for her bridal trousseau.

"So all I am good for is a wife," she thought.

At fourteen, Rebecca was a beautiful child-woman and attracted the stares of men or boys whenever she appeared in public. Her ample bosom focused their eyes, but her face, strong chin, flawless skin, long lashes, and lustrous hair were what stunned them.

To overcome the awkwardness that often accompanied this situation, she had developed the habit of dipping her face when talking to anyone, which was endearing to most. It had the effect of bringing them closer so as to hear more clearly.

Unfortunately for Rebecca, they really didn't want to hear what she said, but instead drank of her beauty.

Unfortunate because she was an intelligent girl who read voraciously and hungered for more experiences beyond the tight household she inhabited.

Her father was a successful merchant, as were his brothers.

The family lived in a pleasant house on Mulberry Lane in Newark.

Each brother had a store along the main street called little more than the broad way. As the city prospered, so did the brothers.

At an early age, her brothers worked in the store when not going to school or studying Hebrew. Even this avenue was not open to her after gaining initiation in the Jewish adult world.

Her mother sensed her unhappiness but did not know what to do. She hoped Rebecca would find a match before she was eighteen.

She never doubted that eligible men would come calling but wondered how Rebecca would handle them.

Her husband had hinted at going to the matchmaker, but she was able to dissuade him.

"Rebecca will find her mate, and if she chooses, he will agree."

Her husband snorted and left the matter to her.

Rebecca was a great reader and spent hours in her room devouring whatever book came her way.

Some she read three or four times. One in particular greatly affected her—Walter Scott's *Ivanhoe.*

The book's Jewish heroine was named Rebecca and sacrificed herself for Ivanhoe.

Her dream was to find a knight like Ivanhoe to rescue her from a lifetime of home chores.

In her heart, she knew this was all but impossible in her world.

What also frustrated her was the knowledge that she was smarter than her brothers but knew she would never be let into the family business.

As she stood serving the men in her home, she followed their conversations. Often, she saw the answer to a problem vexing her father and brothers before they did.

After trying a few times to join the conversation, she learned to be quiet.

More often the not, her solution proved to be the one settled on after much discussion.

In her room afterward, she cried in frustration.

As she grew older, her frustration grew as boys and even some older men started to court her.

When she wanted to talk about current happenings or business, they smiled indulgently and turned to talk about themselves and what they expected of a wife.

Over time, she learned to bite her tongue on these occasions, especially when her mother was within earshot.

On her eighteenth birthday, her mother sat with her.

"It is time you started thinking of marriage."

"It's all I have been thinking about," she lied.

"There are many men who have asked your father about you."

"And many who have tried to hold my hand."

"You must let them, otherwise they will be discouraged."

"I hope I have discouraged a few. They want my body but not my mind."

"It has been so for generations."

"This is America—women work alongside their men."

"Not in our world."

"Perhaps it is time to change that."

"It will not happen in our lives."

"But Mama, they look at me as a piece of meat to be devoured."

"It is how we get what we want by using our bodies to bend them to our needs."

"Then why not become a whore and get what we want without the need to be subservient?"

"You get those ideas from the books you read."

"And from the Bible and Torah."

"You are being profane."

"No, just realistic."

"No man will marry you if you think like that."

"The man I marry will have fresh ideas."

Her mother was aghast at her daughter's words but said nothing to her husband, trusting to events to tame her daughter of these ideas.

When the event did happen it surprised father, mother, and daughter.

Peter Prescott 1832

As he watched his son negotiate with a plow-maker, Peter Prescott was satisfied.

The company he had started thirty-nine years ago was in good hands.

He had done many things good and bad in his lifetime, but the best thing was his son.

Whether selling to or buying from Prescotts, the men who traded with the company were unsure if it was better to deal with the father, Peter, or the son, Henry.

The older man tended to give the better price or other concessions but often cut corners on the payment or delivery.

The younger man drove harder bargains but always kept to the spirit and letter of the deal.

There was another reason other businessmen preferred to deal with the son.

Because of certain things he did in the early part of the nineteenth century, Peter Prescott was tolerated and dealt with but never liked.

By contrast and amongst the men he dealt with, it was said there was no one shrewder or fairer than Henry Prescott. He was therefore from an early age respected and trusted.

Together the two men were the epitome of the successful American merchant in the first half of the nineteenth century.

Peter based his early success on being able to obtain goods in rare supply in America.

He did this despite antitrade laws and English and French attacks on trade as the two belligerent powers waged a worldwide conflict that created shortages in America.

During this turbulent period people bought from Peter Prescott, but when peace returned they forgot their part in these transactions and viewed him as a pariah.

He shrugged off their feelings and built a series of emporiums up and down the Northeast and as far west as Ohio.

Peter's fascination was with making money, not making friends.

His one love was his son, whom he tutored from an early age.

However, he was never friendly or intimate with him, withholding words of love or encouragement, as his father had done to him.

Peter did not see the effect his actions had on his son.

Henry came into the business as a teenager, and by the time he was twenty, he was his father's full partner.

Their customers indicated in many subtle ways their preference for dealing with him rather than his father.

One reason was his youth. At first they tried to out-bargain the younger Prescott but soon found he was a better trader than his father.

They also discovered he struck a hard bargain, whether selling a wagonload of goods, buying a horse, or getting a porch fixed.

This trait was mitigated by a strong sense of obligation once a deal was agreed upon.

This trait perplexed the father, who blamed his wife for their son's honesty.

Henry could never explain this adherence to keeping a bargain, but he accepted it. In his dealings with people, both in business and in his personal life, it was a guiding principle.

His word was his bond, and he made sure it permeated his company. While his father scoffed at this trait, he allowed his son to instill its tenets inside the company.

'It will be your company someday, so do it your way," was his only comment.

Over the years, this adherence to honesty in deal making helped the company survive crisis after crisis.

From the age of seventeen Henry traveled almost constantly, checking on the company's depots, negotiating with suppliers, and learning every aspect of the business.

Shaped by his father to look deep into situations and to store information, he was also naturally curious.

Starting with George Gilbert, and as a result of his observations and travels, he developed a healthy respect for the tinkerers, craftsmen, and inventors who were making things happen in the invigorated American economy of what is called the Jackson period leading up to 1860.

Although father and son worked and lived closely, Peter never told his son how he obtained his goods during the war or from whom.

The father went to his grave never revealing this aspect of the business, nor would he say much about his background and why he came to America, nor provide any information about his roots in England.

"We're Americans now; the past doesn't matter," was the father's usual reply to any questions by the son.

Throughout his life, Henry Prescott occasionally wondered about this but decided in young manhood to accept this secrecy in his father.

His mother was the daughter of a doctor who had lived in the outlying area of Newark all his life, as had his father before him.

Called the Oranges at this time, they were pockets of wealth and poverty. It was not until the later years of the nineteenth century that the towns were incorporated into what were East Orange, Orange, and West Orange.

But the hamlets had streets; muddy lanes, really, that were divided into good and bad sections.

A hardware store owner built a string of houses along a plot that would be Elmwood Street, named for the stately elms that grew in more or less a straight line. These trees survived until the middle of the twentieth century, when they succumbed to Dutch elm disease.

She was intelligent but early on learned to accept she would learn nothing about her husband's past.

They met on a village street while Peter was visiting a merchant in her hometown.

For Peter, one look was enough.

He ardently courted her despite her parents' objection.

Just eighteen, Penelope Richards had a mind of her own, and the intrigue in Peter's background attracted her.

They married in her Episcopal church with only her family and friends in the pews.

Penelope came to realize Peter had few if any friends.

Peter had a house and office, which she moved to with her dowry of furniture and other household goods.

He built an addition to the house for her and quietly suggested she remain in while he conducted business.

It set the pattern of their lives, she running the household and raising the children, he conducting his business and life as he wanted it to be.

Penelope devoted her life to her children and her church.

In the years of her marriage, he never brought one friend for dinner or a social evening.

His vagueness about his background remained another secret between them.

Only Henry survived childhood, for which she had regrets.

A much-loved daughter died of dysentery at the age of five.

Another son died under the wheels of a wagon while playing in front of their house.

Smallpox took her parents in the 1820s, and one brother moved to Ohio, becoming a mayor of Cincinnati.

Her other brother was a doctor, but he and his family were not friendly to Peter.

As a result, she focused her life on her husband and surviving son and the church.

Peter joined her Episcopal church and attended Sunday services with her and contributed generously to its upkeep, but he had little use for religion. He scandalized many neighbors by working on Sunday, a habit he passed on to his son.

Throughout his life, Peter focused on his business, sparing time only for his wife and children.

But even here, there was a remoteness about him, and while father and son shared many things, emotional closeness was not one of them.

Henry knew his father loved him, but there were no outward or spoken bands of love.

He regretted this and turned for emotional support to his mother.

As a result, Henry had his father's insularity and his mother's inner warmth. This warmth was seldom displayed, shaping a very complex man ideally suited to growing a great enterprise.

When only Henry survived childhood, his father focused his being on his son.

Henry in turn had a strong devotion to his father, but because he knew the man held secrets, there was a reserve built up in his inner soul that permeated his entire life.

Henry Prescott 1834

It was business that brought Henry Prescott to his first meeting with Rebecca Zimmerman.

As a businessman who defined himself by his mercantile success, Henry was focused on one thing—making money

The two Prescotts sold to Jews, Catholics, and anyone else who had the money to buy their goods.

Through his business dealing and at an early age he was thrust into many different cultures.

Among the company's local customers were the Jews of Newark. By the time of Andrew Jackson's presidency there was a very strong community living in the largest city in the state.

Because of his own filial coldness, the strong family bonds in Jewish culture both attracted and, in a way he did not understand, repelled him.

However, since Henry made it his business to know as much as possible about the men he dealt with and because of his natural curiosity, he asked to join some of their family occasions.

It was at one of these events in 1835 that he first saw Rebecca Zimmerman at a Newark, New Jersey bar mitzvah, where he was the only non-Jew present.

At the celebratory luncheon, he first saw Rebecca across the room and was struck by her robust figure. He moved closer, looked over a man's shoulder, and saw her face. The first thing he noticed was that she looked out at the world through eyes made more intense by long lashes.

Moving behind her, while appearing not to be interested, he intently listened to her conversations. He noted her flirtatious ways but also recognized from her words that indicated she hid an agile mind. The men spoke of little things but she asked probing questions. These questions were couched in an earnest manner but seemed to elicit condescending answers.

As the conversations continued a note of annoyance crept into her words.

Henry saw there was an impatience there under the polite manner that she barely hid from an acute listener or observer.

The men she talked with seemed not to notice anything about her but her figure and face.

Henry noted that when her mother drew near, she switched to a more flirtatious banter.

He attributed this tactic to her being stifled somewhat by her traditional parents. Henry sensed that they expected her to be a dutiful wife, while she wanted something more from life.

When talking, she had a habit of dipping her head and looking upward into a man's face. This attracted some of the younger men, none of whom seemed to fully grasp her need for meaningful conversation.

With her mother nearby, he noted how she flirted decorously with them, laughing and smiling at them while putting them at ease but keeping them at a distance.

He suspected her family did not quite appreciate the mind hidden by her beauty and the fact she was a woman.

She captivated Henry, who felt her intense emotions hidden by her flirtatious laugh and seemingly open face. He in turn felt a strong attraction to her as a woman. This was a new feeling for him and he felt his manhood stirring in a way no other woman had ever affected it.

When her mother move away, seemingly satisfied her daughter was behaving in the manner expected of her, he swung around in front of her.

Surprising himself, he stared into her face.

Rebecca was taken aback by the intensity of his stare. He was looking boldly into her eyes like no man had done before. She didn't drop her head but stared boldly back.

"Your cousin is very serious," he said of the boy who was celebrating his bar mitzvah.

"He's the one chosen to be a rabbi," she replied.

"Do all in your family have roles given them?"

"Yes, we are all given our roles."

"And yours?"

"To be a dutiful wife."

"Is that what you want?"

"In our world, women have few choices."

"What would you like to be?"

"An adventurer."

"Marriage is an adventure."

"Not for women. Their role is to stay home and have babies."

"It is important to men to have children and wives to look after them."

"But they have no regard for what women want."

"If I married you, I would expect you to stay home and take care of the children."

"I would not marry you with those conditions."

"Under what conditions would you marry me?"

"That we would be partners in life."

"My father would not like for me to have partners."

"From what my father says, you are the real driver in Prescotts."

"So, you have heard about me."

"It is the talk of this bar mitzvah. You practically invited yourself."

"I want to learn about your traditions. We do a lot of business with Jews, and I want to understand your people."

"An unusual goal for a gentile."

"The more I know, the better I will be at dealing with people."

"That is what we tell our children."

"That is what I would tell my children."

"Children are a man's legacy."

"As are they to the mother that gave them birth and to the marriage that produced them."

"Why do you talk of marriage? Are you thinking of marriage?"

"I had not thought much about it until I saw you."

Rebecca was a little startled by the directness of the handsome man in front of her. In many ways he fit the picture of the man she dreamed of marrying. The fact he was a gentile was of no importance to her. She thought for a moment, her head down as she often held it when thinking before others. What came out of her mouth was not in her mind.

"You flatter me, but I do not believe you."

"I will always tell you the truth."

"What makes you think I believe you now or will see you again?" she said in a rush.

"Because you are the most beautiful woman I have ever seen."

"What a liar, and when you just told me you would always tell me the truth."

"No, I really think you are the most beautiful woman I have ever seen. That is the truth."

"But why do you think we will meet again?"

"Because it is what I want and hope you do as well."

"You speak foolishness. We are in separate worlds."

"But breathe the same air. See the same sun. Drink the same wine."

"Is it the wine that is talking now?"

"No, it is what my feelings for you are saying."

Rebecca had not been so ardently wooed before and was out of her element. She dipped her head again and thought about what was being said. In so doing, the top of her head briefly touched his breast, and his hand came up quickly and touched her hair. His touch electrified her, and she abruptly pulled away.

Some in the crowd saw the exchange and murmured their disapproval.

The couple ignored them, their world collapsed into a tiny space around them in the large hall.

"May I see you again?"

"My parents would not like it."

"Would you?"

"I think so."

"Then I will call on you next Sunday."

"No, I will meet you in the park."

"I will not start our relationship with a lie. I will come by your house at two, and we will walk to the park openly."

She looked up at him.

"For a husband and wife, truth is the bond," he said, and she did not demur.

"That's a good start if we are to be true to each other."

He left her there bemused but strangely excited.

Henry came to her house and picked her up. Both ignored the stares of her parents and they spent the afternoon together.

He did this every Sunday for two months.

Their conversations became more intimate, delving into subjects like business and books, and gradually a warm relationship grew.

She was surprised by how little learning he had but pleased by his questioning ways.

Denied school after an early age, Rebecca was a prolific reader, at eighteen still seeing life in romantic ways but with a strong streak of common sense.

He was mesmerized by her ability to see people as they really were. They discovered that they looked at life in many of the same ways.

His honesty impressed her, as did his gradual admission of fears and ambition.

For Henry truly feared failure. It was so a part of his character that it drove his daily life. No matter how much money he made, it would never assuage his fear of failure.

Opening up to someone and seeking a deeper relationship was new to both of them. They were tentative and bold at the same time, creating a special relationship that would span decades.

They talked of business, what was important to each of them, their cultures, their religions, their hopes, and of what the future might be.

Rebecca displayed knowledge of his business world that surprised and delighted him.

She noted the surprise and thought of all the times she had listened quietly while the men in her family discussed business, oblivious to her presence.

All her life, Rebecca had listened to what her father, brothers, and cousins said about their workaday lives.

They never took the time to find out that she had an acute sense of people. She hid this and much more from everyone but Henry.

Their walks were punctuated by intense embraces. When he kissed her, she responded eagerly. He in turn came away from each encounter eager for more. She did as well.

Without much experience in these matters, each learned to explore their physical feelings with each other.

Since women talk more about their sexual urges and what happens in the marriage bed, she was a little wiser than Henry.

His experiences were with pleasure women, his father having brought him to an establishment on his eighteenth birthday in New York City. It was quick and unsatisfying but exciting. Subsequent trips up until he met Rebecca gave him a fuller knowledge of the act, but not of the relationship that made it more fulfilling.

They both recognized that there was an intense sexual feeling each had for the other.

For the first time in his life, Henry found himself neglecting his work while thinking of her during the week.

His father saw the change but said nothing. His mother began to resign herself to the fact that a Jew was going to join the family. It hurt her.

Slowly and without conscious reflection, Rebecca came to love Henry for his strength and honesty.

She held back her love, because to experience it she would need to turn her back on her religion and family.

In these months, he gradually told her more and more about what he did when he was away from her. This was something he never did before, and at some place deep in his being it frightened him.

Prescotts, father and son, were not people who shared. To Henry, this harboring of secrets was instilled almost from birth. Sharing with this woman took great courage on his part. But once he shared one thing with her, he began to tell her more and more.

To his surprise, her responses and observations were acute and often paralleled his own inclinations.

They crossed some point on one walk in early September when he told her of his plans for the future—something he had not even discussed with his father.

"I intend to build a great mercantile company from what my father has started," he said to her as they lay in the grass on Knowland's Knoll, a popular walking place for young couples.

He had spread his coat to allow her to sit in the grass.

"It will stretch to the Mississippi River and north and south from here," he continued.

"Others have tried and failed since Jacob Astor started the American Fur Company," she replied.

"That is because he tried to grow too fast and too far."

"And you don't intend to do that?"

"No, we will grow one step at a time. Moving forward one emporium at a time."

"What is an emporium?"

"A bigger general store that sells to customers and other merchants."

"How will you manage this great enterprise?"

"With your help."

Gradually, they came to an agreement and understanding, She would not be the traditional wife he always imagined he would marry. It was easier than she thought, for in truth, he had given little thought about marriage until meeting her.

She decided to defy her parents and marry him when he finally voiced something he had said at their first meeting and had mulled over since the second month of his courtship.

"I want you as my wife. But to have you I need to make you my partner for life. I realize with my father getting older, I will be away and busy most of the time. It is what I am. I need a companion whom I can trust and love," he told her during one of their walks.

"You know I won't be shut away and viewed as a brood mare."

"No, I will cherish you, and we will together build a dynasty."

"You will take our children and make them like yourself."

"Only if they want to be. Like my mother, you will be our anchor."

"I will be giving up a great deal of my heritage."

"But you will gain a whole new world."

"You make it sound so exciting."

"What we will do will be exciting."

"You will need to ask my father."

"It will probably cost me his business."

"But you will gain me."

"A fair exchange."

Her father was aghast when he asked for permission to marry her and even angrier when she said that was her wish too.

No one in the family, least of all her father, knew she had read *Ivanhoe* as a young girl and was determined from an early age to marry a non-Jew. One of the heroines of Walter Scott's narrative was named Rebecca, and she sacrificed herself for Ivanhoe.

What could be more romantic for a cloistered, intelligent woman with little access to the outside world?

Henry Prescott was an ideal choice for a nineteen-year-old woman who dreamed of a life beyond the Jewish world.

He was tall and blue-eyed, and he came from a family of merchants, much like her father's family.

While Henry agreed to a Jewish wedding, he also required that they marry in his Episcopal church as well.

To the horror of her family and friends, Rebecca did not object when he also required their firstborn William and their other children to be baptized and brought up in his faith.

She in turn demanded his first name be Abraham after her dead grandfather.

Throughout his life, he was known as William but signed his name A. William Prescott.

To their regret, William was the only baby boy to survive childhood. A sister succumbed to an infection and a brother died of diphtheria.

Rebecca lavished much attention on William, but as he grew to manhood she saw him becoming very definitely his father's son.

They lived as a contented couple until her death in 1875. He remained in the house, dying there in 1903.

On their honeymoon to a hotel in Elberon, New Jersey, she gave herself to him so completely he was almost overwhelmed.

When she began to go into the bathroom, he stopped her.

"Undress in front of me. It will be our first time, and I want to see you as you are."

She did not hesitate but peeled off her garments one at a time until she stood naked in front of him.

He looked at her by the dim light of the oil lamp and was astonished at her beauty,

Henry picked her up and carried her to the bed. He laid her down on the coverlet and undressed quickly. Standing before her, his manhood aroused, he plunged on top of her and painfully entered her.

She thrust up to meet him, feeling his manhood inside her for the first time, and cried out.

Her cries encouraged him, and he drove even deeper into her.

His ejaculation came as a crescendo of ecstasy was still building for her. He lay on top of her, with feelings he never had before.

Within minutes, he found himself aroused by her kisses and plunged back into her. This time he was longer and gentler. She climaxed as he finished, and they laid together on the still-made bed.

The got under the coverlet and mated twice more that night.

In the morning, after a few hours sleep, they made love again, each glorying in the other's body.

He had breakfast brought to the room, and over the remains of their meal they made love again.

For three days, they barely left the room. When they did, they walked along the beach arm in arm. On the third day, they attended a concert but left midway to have sex again.

Both took delight in their lovemaking, exploring each other's bodies with an abandonment neither had known before.

She was happy with the man she married, and he was enthralled with her.

Their honeymoon set the pattern for their life together behind their bedroom door.

Throughout their lives, sex was a thing for them alone, and he never strayed from their bed.

Their married life was one of intimate exchanges in their bed, where he often talked about his business and his doubts.

On the last day of their honeymoon, he gave her an emerald necklace he had had specially made for her.

It was the most extravagant gift he ever bought, but not the last jewelry he gave her.

On special occasions, or after long absences, he would find some bauble to give her.

Normally parsimonious in his spending habits, Henry showered his wife with jewelry in the years of their marriage.

Often, when receiving one of his gifts, she would say she had more jewelry than she could ever wear. One of the heartbreaks of her life was that no daughter lived to receive this bounty.

Over time, the collection proved to be a rich treasure, and its dispersal through the generations elicited some family arguments.

On special occasions, in their bedroom, she would wear the necklace and nothing else. It aroused Henry every time.

Throughout their marriage she encouraged him to do more, and she held him in her arms when bad things happened. She came to understand the complex man who dealt honorably with people, but who was perpetually surprised when they did not reciprocate.

Her native intelligence often helped him to see things in others that he blinded himself to.

Until their eldest son matured into his partner, Henry relied on her for advice and comfort.

She nursed her children but saw all but two die before their teens.

This was the heartbreak of her life, and one that was never quite assuaged.

Henry Prescott 1839

Saturday dinners at the Prescott home served two purposes.

For Henry Prescott, they gave him an opportunity to advance his business dealings.

For his wife, Rebecca, it was a chance to reconnect with her family and to exercise her mind talking to the businessmen and out-of-town visitors who regularly came to these dinners.

Today's gathering included her mother, father, and one brother, along with a cousin who was a rabbi.

There were other people at the table set, so Rebecca was opposite her husband, and he could see her clearly without moving his head.

It was the first Saturday in May 1839, and her scoop-neck green velvet dress was accessorized with the emerald necklace that was her wedding gift from her husband.

Whenever she noticed him looking at her, she touched it lightly, reminding him of her devotion to him.

As he often was, Henry found himself aroused by the sight of his wife Rebecca presiding over the table and speaking quietly to the man at her right, occasionally turning to the left to talk to her father.

She touched his hand often, reassuring him of her love and happiness with her life.

He was ill at ease at these gatherings, even though his personal wealth was probably more than the other men seated at the table with the possible exception of her father.

Rebecca was his favorite daughter, but her decision to marry a gentile still baffled and hurt him.

Usually, he came to the first of these dinners each month, always taking one of his sons with him for support.

His daughter was careful to have separate food served to her family so as not to violate Jewish dietary law.

She noted her brother Hyman ate the ham despite his wife's disapproving look.

In their time, the main meal of the day was held in the afternoon and was called dinner.

Since their marriage, this weekend gathering was a time important to both of them.

Because they did it in concert and with much thought beforehand as to whom to invite, it helped to cement their partnership, which grew each day.

Today's gathering was a case in point.

She was speaking to the local banker, who was there in order to advance his proposal that Henry and his father, Peter, invest in his bank.

Henry studied the man and decided he disliked him for the pompous ass he was.

Still, father and son had already decided to put their money with the man—but they would supervise him closely.

The banker, aptly named Amos Cashman, was clearly doing his best to impress Rebecca.

Henry had found most men who first met her eyed his wife for her beauty were then always surprised by her quick mind.

Outgoing and vivacious, she was a sharp contrast to his guarded, reserved nature.

Some said they were a mismatched couple, but he knew better.

As a couple, they made a formidable duo, both in business and in the marital bed.

Across the table he looked at her. To him and others, Rebecca was beautiful—made more so by the slight roundness her body took on after bearing two children.

Tall, with firm, melonlike breasts and widening hips that always eagerly thrust up to meet him when they made love, Rebecca acted decorously now, as she always did in public.

There was another side to her that only he knew.

Sitting there at the ornate table created for him by a craftsman who had been a slave for George Washington, Henry yearned to caress the sexual animal she became in their bedroom.

He wanted the dinner to end so he could take her to bed, first in a ferocious coupling and then in a more leisurely manner during the afternoon lull that followed these weekly gatherings.

Not a particularly demonstrative man and brought up in a household with a cold father but a loving—albeit retiring—mother, Henry was a hard man who hid a generous nature behind the facade of a flinty, successful mercantile leader.

His passion was his work. This informed his everyday existence until he met Rebecca.

In fact, he had not even thought of marriage until he met her.

From the moment he saw her, he wanted to possess her.

To his continuing surprise, Rebecca—the sexual partner who stirred him at times like this—also brought him a social and family life he had never thought he needed. For this he was grateful.

These dinners were a concession he made to her in the early days of his marriage.

At first, he suffered these dinners because of her. Over time, his attitude changed, and he was forced to admit to himself that their guests often proved interesting and helpful to his business ventures.

That they proved helpful to his business affairs was something of an added profit. His true reward came afterward in their afternoon trysts, which often lasted until dark.

To Henry, the drive for success was all-consuming. He knew no other passion except possessing his wife's body, which drove him so completely.

Each Saturday, their house was a gathering place for a disparate group of visitors. There were Jews, some of whom were Rebecca's family members who came at her invitation after temple. Also present were Christian businessmen who dealt with his company and their wives.

Often times, these Christians were meeting Jews in a social setting for the first time.

Many people were surprised that Henry had chosen to marry a Jewish woman.

It surprised him as well.

His father, who founded the business in the early part of the century, said nothing except that it would cost the firm money if her family objected to the marriage.

The Christian families were often there at his invitation, and they seldom refused the chance of diminishing his rich table. There were always two or three meats, mounds of side dishes, and rich desserts.

Henry enjoyed good food and personally hired the women who acted as cooks in the house. His mother was a plain cook and willingly gave up that chore while Henry was still a child. The succession of cooks she hired provided ordinary fare, and when he turned twenty-one, he demanded and got the right to find good cooks.

Throughout his life, what he ate at home was important to him.

When he married, he continued the practice, and Rebecca did not demur. She did not like to cook and was happy to leave the chore to others.

Ironically, few people ever saw this side of him, assuming this household chore was overseen by Rebecca.

What many saw in these social settings was a different side to him, for here he was more outgoing then in his business dealings. To be sure, it was only an act he put on to please his wife and to advance his interests.

Occasionally a doctor, minister, or rabbi would also be there.

Today there was an elderly Negro present at the table. He was ill at ease at the occasion but tried gamely to fit in.

Henry looked at him with great affection.

He thought back to the first time he met George Gilbert.

No one at the table knew he was born a slave on George Washington's estate. Nor did they know the table and chairs they occupied were built by him.

George Gilbert lived in the Negro section of the suburban enclaves commonly called the Oranges at this time. His workshop was four muddy lanes a world removed from the Prescott mansion.

He settled there after being freed by the first president's will. Unlike many former slaves who stayed on the estate at Mount Vernon, Gilbert left immediately, settling in East Orange because he liked the name, and because there was already a group of manumitted slaves there.

His skill as a furniture builder enabled him to feed and clothe his wife and five children.

He sold his custom-made furniture mainly to local residents, but occasionally visitors would remark on the quality and have something made for them.

Sometimes these visitors would forget to pay him when he sent them the pieces, convincing George Gilbert to limit his trade to townspeople. He wasn't rich and lived day to day, but he and his family were happy.

On this day they were joined by a writer of travel books and the minister of Henry's Episcopal church, which was just four blocks or squares from his home.

The minister and rabbi were seated together, apparently getting along, an unusual occurrence in this era.

His father Peter was also there, but in his old age he seemed somewhat out of place.

Peter founded the family business, but Henry had driven its growth since joining him.

Henry's formal education ended at fourteen, and he was almost a full partner by the time he was seventeen.

While the conversation was always lively, Henry took little part in these discussions, only interrupting to ask a question. Rebecca usually led the discussions. He preferred to listen, often amused as visitors were surprised by Rebecca's range of knowledge and interests.

When he was drawn into a conversation he seldom voiced an opinion.

As with many men of his generation, his knowledge came from doing and from learning from other people.

Henry knew Rebecca had given up much to marry him. She moved away from the day-to-day contact with her family, leaving the Jewish enclave in Newark to settle two hours or more away.

At this point, their marriage was entering its fifth year, and his lust for her still surprised him.

She turned from the banker at her left and caught his eye. Rebecca smiled to herself; she knew the look in his eyes. She dipped her head like she always did when looking out at the world and widened her smile for him. Her face returned his carnal look, giving him reassurance of her need for him. Satisfied he had got her message, she swiveled her head back to the writer at her right and started to converse with him.

The minister and rabbi on Henry's right noted the exchange and said nothing.

The other men's conversation was focused on the controversy concerning the national bank, which was a recurring issue of the day.

The banker Cashman was present that day, anxious for the Prescott investment, and he was doing his best to impress Rebecca. Like others, he knew she was more than a stay-at-home wife but rather took an active role in Henry's business affairs.

He was hoping to get her help in getting Henry to invest in the bank.

In the past two years, the Prescotts, father and son, had become his biggest depositor.

He was afraid they would move their business to a bigger bank, and he knew that if they left his financial institution, it would be in trouble.

Father and son were only debating how to best secure their investment and how much they would ultimately decide to invest. Like the shrewd businessmen they were, they were keeping Cashman dangling.

Later that day, Henry would ask Rebecca's opinion of the banker. If she strongly demurred, he would not invest.

In this little example, he realized how much of the business was falling into his hands, and how dependent he was on his wife's counsel.

Peter was clearly failing in health, and more and more he differed with his son in many matters.

Henry's inquisitive mind and uncanny business sense were driving the business.

Despite his presence at these gathering, he still held back on making friends or easy conversation. When pressed, he fell back on his penchant for asking questions.

Early in his life, he inherited his father's reserve and a poker-face approach to life.

Added to this trait was a desire to know everything about something he was involved in.

Whenever Henry decided to do something, he learned as much as possible about the situation. He did this by questioning the people he met or did business with.

Some men resented this about him. Cashman in particular resented it and promised himself he would cut the Prescotts out once he had the money.

That was why they were learning everything they could about banking before investing.

Already, they had seen things at the local bank they did not like and would press Cashman to change before investing.

Although Henry was not a naturally gregarious person, he did have the ability to draw out people, particularly when that person was knowledgeable about a subject he was interested in learning more about.

As they had agreed beforehand, Rebecca spent much of the dinner quietly talking to the bank president. By the time dessert was served, he knew she would find out enough to help him protect their investment.

Today's other guests did not particularly interest him. Rather, he was picturing his wife naked on their bed.

He chafed a little as dessert was served; this social gathering was getting in the way of his carnal desires, and he was a little put out.

By four o'clock the guests were gone, and he went upstairs to their bedroom. Their house was built for the conducting of business while protecting the privacy of its owners.

Rebecca was there already, undressing quietly as he entered the room.

He looked at her as she shed her garments, marveling at her body as each part was revealed.

She stood there naked for a moment and walked languidly to the bed.

He dropped his clothes on the floor and strode quickly to the bed.

It was a large bed, specially made by George Gilbert. (At auction at the beginning of the twenty-first century, it sold for more than $100,000.)

These were the intimate moments he loved best—when they looked at each other.

Their lovemaking was like a renewal of the ties that bound them almost from the first moment they met.

They were a couple who enjoyed and respected each other.

When they were alone, the world was left outside, and they had eyes and thoughts only for each other. Their marriage worked despite their differences and, truth be told, both were surprised and pleased by their choices of mate.

Their lovemaking was just part of a partnership that extended into all aspects of their lives.

Henry had no other intimate friend or advisor.

Rebecca lived for her husband and his work.

While her children were important, they took second place to the man who now drove inside her body.

She was aroused by his lovemaking and let herself go as he pounded into her.

He often took her without a word or a kiss.

She accepted that and responded to him, knowing his second and third time would be gentler and more caring.

She stifled any cries and clung to him, not usually coming until their second mating.

On occasion she clawed into his back with her nails, and she noticed that when she did, he ignored the pain in the heat of his passion.

Except for soft words when alone, they never outwardly demonstrated their love for each other, but no one who met them doubted their commitment to the marriage.

As a result, outsiders often said, "Neither was shortchanged in the bargain they made with each other."

Intermarriage between Christian and Jew was not a common occurrence at this time.

Both families were aghast at the marriage, and both had reservations.

Henry's father said nothing beyond speculating about the loss of business when told of his son's choice. His mother, a devout Christian, was appalled.

Her parents cried and wondered where they had they gone wrong in their child-rearing.

Her siblings never fully accepted Henry or their children.

The marriage worked not only because of what happened behind their bedroom door, but also because he trusted her as he did no one else in his life.

When alone together in their bedroom, he could drop the need to be strong and decisive.

Here Henry could admit his deficiencies and fears.

She in turn could be the woman who explored her innermost sexual cravings while also acting as sounding board, helpmate, and partner.

Together they built the foundation of what would be a great enterprise.

As they made love that afternoon, neither thought of anything else.

They came down to supper sated and happy.

As usual, they were joined by his parents, who said little.

His mother was a devout Episcopalian, but religion matter little to Henry.

Her friends at church clucked at the introduction of this Jewish woman into their society.

Religion was not an important part of Henry's life.

However, because religion played such a role in this society, the family regularly attended the local Episcopal church.

Henry never noticed the stares of fellow churchgoers when the family took its place in the front pew of the church.

Rebecca saw but said nothing, feeling somewhat estranged.

Necessarily distant from her own religion and culture at this point in her life, she accepted the consequences of her decision to marry Henry.

She had made her bargain and was satisfied she had gotten good value.

Peter Prescott 1840

As he lay dying, Peter Prescott was confident his business would survive.

He smiled at the thought he was dying in a house his son had constructed, and in which his wife and he were really guests.

He sensed that his wife Penelope was not happy in the house but assuaged his guilt by knowing she would be well provided for by her son.

Peter left everything he owned to his son, charging him with providing for his mother.

This was not an uncommon occurrence at this time.

Perhaps better than his son realized, Peter knew his offspring well.

"He's a shrew businessman, but he has a heart."

Peter also approved of his daughter-in-law.

"There's no softness in her except for my son; she'll help achieve more," was his summation.

Of his grandchildren Peter was not sure, because they were still young.

He thought of telling his son more of his background but put it away quickly.

"Let sleeping dogs lie," was his excuse.

They had moved from their house to the house on Elmwood Street when Henry and Rebecca were married in 1835.

In her lifetime Penelope lived only three places, and in none was she ever fully in control. This seemed not to matter to her, but in fact it was the source of a lifelong sense of sorrow.

After Henry convinced his father of the utility and economy of merging offices and the two households, she left the running of the household to Rebecca.

Mother-in-law and daughter-in-law came to an understanding, reflecting the generational change as Henry assumed almost total control of the business.

Penelope saw the decline in her husband's vitality, accelerated by his gradual retirement from the business and a lingering cough that presaged his death.

Peter laughed at himself.

"I'm dying in a house that is not even my own."

That thought was succeeded by another.

"It's my son's house, and he is what I will leave this earth. It will be enough."

He realized he had never said how proud he was of him.

"Too late now," Peter thought.

Another thought struck him.

"I've never really told my wife how much I loved her."

He reviewed his life, remembering when he first saw her. He loved her from that moment but never really told her how much.

He wondered if he should tell her now. Again, the thought was dismissed from his mind.

Now, Peter knew his time on earth was drawing to a close.

He looked at the people in his room—his wife, son, and daughter-in-law. They were there to see him die, and he was about to oblige them.

"It was a good life," he murmured to his wife.

"I love you," she said.

He denied her a last chance to hear his love for her and passed away.

Henry Prescott 1840

While walking down the stairs from his father's death chamber, Henry Prescott realized the enormity of the responsibilities he now had. He walked into the office he shared with his father, knowing that from now on it was his chamber alone.

Rebecca came to his side and put her hand on his shoulder.

"He's at peace now," she said.

"But now all this is mine, and I need to make it work."

"We will make it much more than it is now."

"Do you really think so?"

"I know you, and I know what you're capable of."

"I know, but I always felt he was there behind me."

"You ran away from him many years ago. Prescotts is really you. No, I mean us, because I will be your anchor."

"I said that to you when we first met."

"I remember that and everything else you said that day."

"It is really just us now."

"Yes, just us, but now you must go upstairs and comfort your mother."

The funeral was a somber affair attended by employees, Rebecca's parents, and business associates.

She noted that there was not one friend of Peter's there.

They came back to the house, and in the months that followed, its inhabitants saw little changed except that Penelope kept to her rooms, joining them for meals but mostly keeping to herself.

She reduced her time at the church and had little interest in her grandchildren.

"She is pining for your father," Rebecca said one night.

"It's funny but I cannot remember an affectionate word between them in all my life."

"Your father was not a caring man, but in his way he loved her."

"I know he never strayed from her."

"I think the business was all he cared about. The business and you."

"I wonder if it would have been different if my brother and sister had lived?"

"I doubt it—you are the future of Prescotts and he knew it."

"I wonder what we can do for her?"

"Very little; she will either survive or die quickly."

"I hope not. She showed me much love, perhaps trying to make up for my father."

"We are all shaped by our parents."

"I don't think that was the case with you."

"No, I think it was the books I read, and the boys and men I had to suffer."

"I am happy you allowed me to marry you."

"I had no choice; you were the only one who saw I had a mind and a body."

"Speaking of which, your breast is peeking out at me, and it's getting a reaction."

"We mustn't disappoint."

Penelope joined her husband within a year, and these members of the next generation occupied the house by themselves until their son brought home his bride years later.

The house Henry built was to remain the center of Prescott life for seventy-odd years, housing three generations, but it was ultimately abandoned upon Henry's death in 1903.

Built of solid oak timber, with a center hall reception area, the house was designed by Peter to be really two units.

The company's office occupied the lower-half floor to the right.

The parlor and dining room were to the left, but with the company growing, after Rebecca died the entire floor was devoted to the business.

The kitchen and spaces for other domestic functions were relegated to the back of the house.

Spacious and compartmentalized, it could for the most part allow two families to coexist in the house without impinging on each other.

Like many houses of this era, there was a front porch to shelter visitors from the rain and sun while they waited to enter. In the

Prescott house, there were extra chairs for the many businessmen who came regularly to see the Prescott father and son.

None of the Prescott family was ever seen on the porch. The children played in the backyard, especially after one child was run over in front of the house.

The two Prescott women, mother-in-law and daughter-in-law, preferred to remain inside, the older woman upstairs and Rebecca in the office with her husband.

New visitors often showed their surprise at her presence in the business side of the house. They quickly learned she was a functioning member of the business. One or two chided the men working there, but her stern look soon put a stop to that.

It was not just a family home, but served well as the seat of the business and what social life they had, most of which was connected to their enterprise.

This was Henry's plan from the beginning, and it would work well for the next generation.

Their house was on Elmwood Street, which was the most fashionable street of a then-fashionable town.

For much of the nineteenth century, it was said that this section of the Oranges was a quietly rich enclave with an elite group of families centered around Elmwood Street.

The more prosperous inhabitants of Elmwood Street did not flaunt their wealth but rather lived behind the large front porches and gabled windows.

By World War II it had become a warren of divided habitants going to squalor.

Those prosperous inhabitants socialized but did not mingle with the Prescotts. Because they were half-Jewish, the Prescott children had few friends among the other young people on the four blocks that formed Elmwood Street.

They had interaction with their cousins in Newark, but because they were raised as Christians, they kept somewhat apart from many family gatherings.

This reinforced the family trait of looking inward for support and friendship.

The Oranges at this time were an outpost of both Newark and New York City.

Peter and Henry liked it this way, concentrating their efforts in other states.

Their far-flung locations were as easily reached from the New Jersey town as from the cities.

It also forced potential clients and goods providers to come to them, an advantage they utilized in their dealings.

Transportation involved a trip by horse and buggy, then to a ferry to New York City.

For most of nineteenth century, there were sections of the Oranges that were centers of wealth, and residents preferred staying in town.

As industries grew up around them, the Prescotts eschewed changing their location for many years.

Not so their neighbors, who gradually shifted their business locations to the cities.

As a result, it became a commuter town long before that term was coined.

It was not by accident that when the railroad was built, a station was located just five blocks from Elmwood Street.

The Erie Lackawanna station built in 1875 to connect the small suburban city with New York was ornate and designed for a certain class of traveler.

By 1880, most of its male leaders worked in Newark, but many traveled daily to New York City. This number would grow, and eventually the Prescotts would move, first to a building on Main Street, and eventually across the river to offices, homes, and apartments along Park or Fifth Avenue.

Rebecca Prescott 1842

After seven years of marriage, Rebecca Prescott was still learning things about her husband.

That she loved him more today than when they married was without question.

Henry was a complex man driven to build a large mercantile business and to participate in the growing entrepreneurship that characterized the early national period.

She was his only confidant, sharing his bed and his business.

His other love was reserved for his son, William. From the moment he was born in December 1836, Henry focused his life around the twin suns of mother and son. His other children meant little to him, and their deaths would not shake his focus on his son.

Rebecca wisely dissuaded him from adding "& son" to the family enterprise when William was five years old.

"You're founding a dynasty that will live for generations," was her rejoinder.

Often, William would sit on his father's knee in the big office on the first floor of their home and listen with rapt attention as his father read and explained what the paper in his hand meant.

It pleased Henry that his son seem to enjoy these sessions.

Determined to give his son a better education than he had, he sent him to the new Newark Academy, soon the most prestigious in New Jersey.

Henry was careful not to tell the Reverend Rector Josephus Edicott of William's Jewish mother when enrolling him. By the time Edicott was informed of the dual ancestry, William was part of the school, and Henry had already promised a donation for the chapel.

Edicott put aside his biases and permitted William to stay.

When he "passed out" at fourteen, he was a class leader who demonstrated a remarkable proficiency in mathematics and reading.

His mother was proud on that occasion but silently grieved that he was not also being given religious training at the Newark yeshiva, but rather at the Episcopal church.

Throughout this period, William worked with his father, learning everything he could about the business.

Rebecca took him to her family gatherings until he turned thirteen. Then questions about his religious training proved too embarrassing.

Like his father, religion descended lightly on William's shoulders, a trait that would continue through all his life.

Not lost, however, on William was Henry's adherence to honesty.

Also not lost on William was Henry's ability to bargain.

Henry was a hard bargainer who was not so much loved as respected.

The aloofness that marked his character slowly softened as he matured.

Whenever his son was along at these meetings, the men saw a softer side to him.

Many approved and thought more of Henry.

Over the years, Rebecca took a more active role in the company.

Some Saturdays would find father, mother, and son settled in the big office, each working on different parts of the business.

Henry's reliance on his wife was stronger than ever, and their shared exuberance as the business grew and prospered was only tempered by his continued drive for more.

His mother's death two years earlier left Rebecca the sole mistress of the house.

She made sure Henry's home life was happy.

When he returned home from his frequent absences, he found a serene environment punctured only by their fierce lovemaking.

On the occasions of his travels, she ran the business as well, finding it exciting.

Rebecca also came to be an effective helpmate who could and did act on Henry's behalf.

This was amply demonstrated in 1842, when she averted disaster for Prescotts.

The banker Cashman came to the office on a Tuesday and said the bank needed money quickly to avert a crisis.

"I'm sure you wouldn't understand," he started out.

"Perhaps you can explain it to me," she replied tartly.

""We have a temporary shortage at the bank and need monies to tied us over."

"How much?"

"Five thousand dollars."

"Why?"

"As I said—for depositors, should they demand their monies."

"Why would they demand their money right now?"

"There are rumors our banks and others are going to fail."

"Why are there rumors?"

"Some banks in the city have failed, and the North Newark bank has failed."

"What has that to do with us?"

"Because I have invested money in the North Newark bank."

"Did you tell my husband you were doing that?"

"I was going to tell him at the next board meeting."

"Why did you do it?"

"My brother led the North Newark bank, and he needed cash."

"So you took our money and gave it to your brother?"

"No, to the North Newark bank."

"What did you get in return?"

"A promissory note."

"From a failed bank?"

"Yes, I am afraid so, but rumors are that our bank is in trouble."

"Is it?"

"Not in the least, but people are asking for their monies, and we will be out of cash by tomorrow or Thursday at the latest."

"So, you want Prescotts to advance you money?"

"Yes."

"On what collateral?"

"If the bank fails you will lose all your investment."

"What will you lose?"

"Everything."

"I have the money to give you, but I want you to sign over all your stock and give me your resignation as well."

"But I will have nothing."

"You will have your good name and a job at the bank, but you will no longer control it."

"I can't do that."

"Then the bank will fail."

In the end, Cashman did as she asked, and when Henry returned two weeks later, he found Rebecca in Cashman's office and the owner of the bank.

Cashman committed suicide a year later, and Prescotts had its first bank.

William joined her during this period and learned about banking while tottering around the bank, which stood on Main Street in East Orange for more than one hundred years.

While Cashman and his successors served as bank president, Rebecca ran the bank for eighteen years, giving up interest when the Civil War started.

Meanwhile, because of Henry's travels, the men who worked for him in the lower floor of their house needed to be trusted.

This was difficult for him to accept.

Under his wife's guidance, he learned to build trust and loyalty from and to his employees.

Rebecca's contribution to the success of Prescotts and exemplified the trait of loyalty that permeated the company throughout its existence.

Through their ascent, Prescotts was not only known for its fairness well into the twentieth century, but also for the loyalty of its employees, which was legendary.

Some employees and retainers worked for and with the company for generations, prospering along with the company.

While Henry demanded and expected loyalty from those he employed, he kept meticulous books, developing a system of checks and balances that permeated the family enterprise for most of its existence.

From father to son, the Prescotts instilled a rigorous management of their affairs.

However, this seemingly strong system of controls did not prevent some employees from stealing, and it allowed some catastrophic events to happen that threatened the company.

One other thing was unique about Henry for his time. He encouraged Negros to improve themselves, sponsoring some of them by paying for their education even before the Civil War.

For this he owed much to George Gilbert, a furniture maker and patient man who taught him how to carve wood.

One family in particular, the Gilberts, benefited from this attitude.

In fact, one was to serve in a high-level capacity for more than fifty years.

Samuel Gilbert 1858

Clark Street was in the heart of Orange's Negro neighborhood. The city sheriffs seldom patrolled its dirt streets, and only Dr. William Alexander's house had indoor plumbing. The waste spilled into the backyard, like every other house on the block, but its inhabitants didn't need to go outside to do their business.

Next door, Samuel Gilbert grew up the fourth of five children and the first boy.

No one ever called his mother anything but "Mama."

He thought he was born on December 25, because his mama always said he was her Christmas boy. Sam never learned that she meant the day he was conceived.

His father went north after being freed by the will of George Washington. He had served at Mount Vernon, the national hero's estate, since his birth.

A carpenter and cabinetmaker, he made a good living in East Orange until his death when Gilbert was just three.

There was little money in the household when his father died.

His mother took service in the Prescott household, starting as a scullery maid.

Later in life, she moved up to kitchen helper but did not advance further by the time she died in 1859.

At that point, Gilbert was seventeen by everyone's reckoning, big for his age and—he realized early on—smarter than most other members of his family.

When his mama died, Henry Prescott came to the funeral, the only white face in the crowd. His wife wanted to come, but he felt the neighborhood was not the place for her.

Henry talked with Gilbert's relations but spoke longest with him.

"What are you going to now, young man?" Henry asked.

Gilbert had no answer but stared at the ground.

"Can you read or write?" Henry persisted.

"Yes, sir," was all Gilbert could say.

"Do you wash every day?"

"Only when I have to and to go to church."

"Can you add and subtract?"

"Some."

"I need someone around the house and to follow around young William. Do you want to do this and tell me what he does?"

"I can."

"Good, come by Monday and make sure you wash before you come."

Henry walked away, and Gilbert followed his back with his eyes.

"You want me to spy on your son," he thought.

Like his father, young William was taciturn in making friendships and kept many thoughts to himself.

His mother's parents were awkward around him, and while still quite young, he saw that they favored his cousins at family gatherings.

Being raised a Christian, he thought little of his Jewish heritage.

Of his Jewish cousins, he sensed no kinship, and one or two even resented his appearances at these gatherings.

Henry saw his son needed someone to help him and thought Gilbert would make an ideal companion.

"White boys would want to take advantage of him," was Henry's rationale.

Not a reflective man, Henry did not see anything unusual in his choice of companion for his son.

Over the years, others noted this relationship and wondered about the closeness of the two men.

The next Monday, Gilbert showed up at the back door of the big house and knocked timidly.

"You might as well come in," a young voice said.

Gilbert opened the door and saw a young man sitting at the kitchen table with some ledger books opened in front of him.

"You're my father's spy, so don't dally. I have something for you to do, so come here."

Gilbert turned to the boy and smiled at him.

"Father thinks you're going to tell him everything, but you're not. You're only going to tell him what I tell you to say."

Gilbert looked at the boy and said nothing.

William handed him a composition book and a nub of a pencil.

"Here, add these numbers and see if you come up with the same answer I did."

Gilbert took the book and started to add them standing up.

"Sit down in that chair and do it right."

Gilbert did as he was told and began adding the numbers.

He didn't know what he was adding, but they seem to be cash numbers. Gilbert was smart. His teacher at the school set up by the city to teach Negroes said he had a quick mind, but these figures were hard.

For an hour, Gilbert went over the numbers carefully. Each time he did them, they came to a result different from the number scratched at the bottom in a different hand.

Finally, after the third time he said quietly, "They ain't the same."

William smiled and looked at him.

"I know that. Just wanted to see if you would tell me they're wrong. Now, add these figures and see if I'm wrong again."

Gilbert added the next column and saw they agreed with his number.

"See anything else with those figures?"

Gilbert looked at both sets of numbers. At first glance there appeared to be nothing wrong. He looked at them again, and something didn't look right. He couldn't fetch what it was, but there was something.

"I dunno, but I see something."

William smiled again and put his finger on the middle of the column.

"Every once in a while there's a dip in the numbers. Look again."

Gilbert looked again and saw the pattern.

"These are the receipt numbers for one of our stores in Greenwich, Connecticut."

Gilbert didn't know where Greenwich was but said nothing.

"I've suspected there's something going on there, and now I've got the proof."

Gilbert just listened. He did not know William had secretly taken the ledgers from Henry's office and had spent the early morning hours carefully reviewing them.

Gilbert never found out how William first suspected the thieving, but it was the first of many times he saw the other man's ability to sniff things out of the air.

William got up, opened the ice chest, and reached a container of apple cider. He poured two glasses and gave one to Gilbert.

Gilbert had only tasted cold apple cider twice in his life and never in a white boy's house. Nor had he drunk from a heavy, clean glass like this one.

William sat down again and drank with a smug look on his face.

"First thing we get agreed—you only tell my father the good things I do. Things like this morning, you wait until I tell him. As for some of the other things we're going to do, you never say a word."

Gilbert figured silence was better than arguing and silently resigned himself to the fact this job was not long for him.

William got up, gathered the ledgers, and went toward the front of the house.

"Well, c'mon, we have to go tell Father the bad news."

Gilbert trailed William into the front parlor, where Beatrice, his mama's replacement, was just starting to clean.

"Youse get back into the kitchen, Sam Gilbert, youse don't belong here."

"He does now, Beatrice, so shush you're mouth," William said strongly.

Gilbert silently followed the master's son into the office that fronted the house.

Henry strode in a few minutes later to see William sitting at his desk and Gilbert standing beside him.

"Well, I see you have met even before I could introduce you two."

"I know what you want from Gilbert, but he's my servant now," William retorted.

Henry shrugged and looked at Gilbert, who stared back at him.

"What are you doing with those ledgers?" The father asked.

"Proving a point to me, and I hope to you."

William opened the ledgers to the figures Gilbert and he had just added.

"There's a thief in our Greenwich store, and I think it is Elliott."

William opened the ledgers and put his finger on the column of figures the two young men had examined earlier.

Henry looked at the figures, got a scrap of paper, and jotted some notes. He turned to his son with a neutral expression on his face.

"I say that is interesting, and you think it is Elliott?

"He's the only one there with enough brains to figure out your way of checking the books. I think he has been stealing from us for two years."

Henry noted the word "us" but said nothing.

"So what do *we* do?" he asked his son.

"Why, fire him, of course, and the sooner the better."

"I agree, so go there today and do it," his father said in a neutral tone.

William was startled by his father's seemingly casual statement.

"Do you mean me? Now? Today?"

"You found the stealing, now go do what needs to be done."

William looked at his father for a moment and came to believe this was a test.

"All right, I'll go after breakfast."

"No, go now and take Gilbert with you. Take the gray team, and if you start now, you should get there just as they're ready to close."

Without another word, he motioned to Gilbert, and the two left.

William Prescott 1858

His father's order to fire the people in the Connecticut office surprised and frightened William Prescott. He left his father's office and went to the nearby stable where the company kept its horses and wagons. The man in charge smiled when he asked for his father's team and buggy.

Gilbert followed along quietly, not knowing what to say or do. The two teenagers were on their way without breakfast and with only a vague sense of how to get to their destination. William had not thought to ask for money or provision but as he left the yard, his father handed him a wallet and a basket of food.

Never having ridden in a horse-drawn conveyance and not knowing where to sit, Gilbert hopped on the back of the buggy, but William motioned for him to sit up front.

When they were out of sight of the house, William opened the basket. It contained a tongue, cheese, a loaf of bread, and a bottle of cider. There was also a knife and two cloth napkins.

Hungry and a little scared, William handed the reins to a startled Gilbert and dove into the basket.

Unsure how to handle the reins, Gilbert pulled them up tightly, slowing the horse.

"Give him his head. He'll follow the road while we eat," William said.

Gilbert did as he was told, wondering what he had gotten into with this boy.

William cut the tongue and the bread.

He handed some of the food to Gilbert and began eating his portion.

Gilbert noted both portions were equal.

He held the reins in one hand and ate with the other. There was one pewter cup in the basket and one pottery mug. William took the pewter cup and poured the cider into it. He placed it on the seat and did the same to the mug.

Again, Gilbert saw the portions drawn were about equal.

They ate and drank in silence, each lost in his own thoughts.

This was the first time William was setting out to a company facility without his father. He thought of what he must do, and how he would do it.

Without admitting it to himself, he was scared.

"This is a test, and I don't know what to do," he mused.

Gilbert, who had never been more than two miles from his home, was now going with a white boy through two states and crossing the Hudson. He was scared as well.

They drove to the Hudson River ferry dock located at the foot of the Palisades. The steam ferry ran regularly across the river and had been doing so for ten years. William's experience with the ferry was limited to two trips with his father and to a family visit to New York the year before.

The ferry was loading when they arrived, and they were able to get a position in the middle of the boat. This suited both boys, and the horse seemed to have no difficulty clopping on board, for which they were grateful.

The ferryman eyed the boys, one white and one black, but said nothing. He tried to push up the fare, but William remembered what his father paid and gave him only that amount.

The ferryman looked at the money, looked at William, and said nothing.

As the ferry made its way across the river, both boys felt queasy in the stomach but said nothing to each other.

The horse seemed unconcerned, eating peacefully from the bucket of oats William put around his head.

"The next time you feed him," William said as he showed Gilbert what to do.

Never having been around horses before, Gilbert was a little hesitant about the chore but followed what William did.

When the ferry touched down on Manhattan Island, the boys clamored aboard the buggy and drove off. At this time, the area around the ferry landing was still farmland. The landing stop was just north of what would eventually be Fifty-seventh Street. They drove the winding road east and north toward the upper part of Manhattan, then boarded another ferry, which brought them to the mainland and the Boston Post Road, which ran from New York City through Connecticut and north to Boston.

It was a well-traveled road, and the boys slipped easily into the horse-drawn and pedestrian stream.

Except to give orders, William had said little, but as the hours drew by, he started to ask questions. They were focused on learning about Gilbert.

William had inherited his father's habit of knowing all about people and things.

Gilbert's answers gave him confidence in his companion.

He knew the task ahead of him was going to be difficult, and he started coaching Gilbert on what he was to do.

"Your job is to keep silent and guard my back," he said at one point.

William paused as he said that, realizing that he was on his own for the first time in his life, and that this boy beside him was his only support.

He wondered whether his companion was capable of doing just that.

Less than an hour later he had his answer.

They were moving at a slow, steady pace when a surrey with three men tried to pass them on the road. Because it had rained within the past two days, the road was rutted, and William was keeping to a patch of smooth dirt.

The surrey was having difficulty with the ruts in the road and swayed toward buggy. William's instinct was to drive straight and let the surrey move away. Instead, the driver tried to push them off the smooth patch. William was on the left side of the carriage, nearest the oncoming surrey. As the man tried to push them into the side of the road he raised his whip to strike William. Reacting swiftly, Gilbert grabbed the basket and took the full force of the whiplash on the basket, protecting William. It wrapped around the basket, and Gilbert pulled it toward himself, almost pulling the man out of his seat.

The man cursed and tried to pull it back, but Gilbert held on; the man was off balance and lost the reins of his horse, which veered away from the buggy.

The boy's horse, sensing danger, pulled harder, and they sped ahead of the surrey, aided by the smooth road. The man in the surrey fought to retrieve the reins, but just then they hit a rut, and the vehicle flipped over, spilling the men into the mud.

At a spirited clip, the boys' buggy moved away from the accident.

They peered back at the scene, looked at each other, and laughed, with Gilbert holding the basket with the whip still attached.

William had his answer and the boys drove on to their destination.

William and Gilbert arrived at the Prescott general store and warehouse on the Boston Post Road just before closing time.

Monday was usually a busy day for the emporium, and this day was no different.

William had been there before with his father, but his solo arrival was greeted with some amusement by the four men working there.

Josephus Elliott had worked for the elder Prescott for almost twenty years, working himself up from a stable boy to running one of the most lucrative outposts in the Prescott string.

"What brings you here, Master William?" Elliott said jovially.

"I have some business here and need you to join me in your office."

"There are things I gotta do out here," Elliott said.

"Join me now, Josephus!" William said in the sternest voice he could muster.

Elliott was twice his age and had been a loyal employee, but he followed William into the office.

Not knowing what to do, Gilbert followed, avoiding the stares of the other workers.

Inside the office, William saw the open cash draw with a pile of money sitting in disarray in the trays.

William faced Elliot and said quietly, "You've been stealing from Prescotts, and you're discharged as of today."

Elliot swung around to face the young man and bellowed, "What proof do you have that I would do such a thing?"

"It's all in the numbers. You've been doing it for two years that I'm sure about and probably longer than that."

"Where's the proof?" Elliot said in a louder voice.

"I'm satisfied you've been stealing, and that's enough. You're lucky I don't call the sheriff, so get out."

"If I go, so go my men. One's my cousin, and the others are squiring my daughters."

"Then go, all of you. We don't cheat our customers, and we won't stand for anyone cheating us."

Elliot raised his arm to strike William, but Gilbert instinctively grabbed the arm and held it against the older man's efforts to strike down.

In a moment, he relaxed, smiled, put on his coat, and walked to the front.

"C'mon, men, we're all fired," he said as he walked to the front, knocking over a barrel of nails on the way.

As they slithered across the floor, the men hesitated and then followed him out, grabbing and throwing down shovels, sacks of grain, and cloth bolts on the way.

William was stunned by the actions and just stood there.

Again, by instinct, Gilbert began righting the fallen merchandise.

Momentarily shaken, William looked at the departing men and realized there were one or two other people still in the store.

Prescotts' outposts were part wholesale warehouses and part sales emporiums, with a lot of different goods and parts to act as a farmers' supply depot. Henry was smart enough not to compete with his retail customers and carefully situated his locations so as not to offend his preferred clients, those who served the general public.

There was a merchant in the store, along with a farmer's wife trying to find material for a coming social.

They looked on as he composed himself and followed Gilbert's lead.

"Nothing's changed, folks. Prescotts will be here as long as you will have us," he said.

Inwardly unhappy with what had happened, William served the two remaining visitors while Gilbert was straightening out the merchandise.

His next act was to write a brief letter to his father and have Gilbert post it. Other customers rushed to the store upon hearing the news about the men being fired.

William carefully explained that only Josephus was fired; the other men had quit.

Many customers clucked about his loyalty, but William dealt briskly with them.

He closed the shop promptly at 6:00 PM.

As Gilbert closed the doors and windows, William counted the money in the till and tried to decide what to do.

"It looks like we are here until my father sends some men to take over," he said to a quiet Gilbert.

The two walked down the street to the local stagecoach stop, and William tried to book sleeping accommodations.

Gilbert stood outside while William sought out the proprietor.

"I can give you a sleeping bed, but the nigger gotta sleep in the back barn," the thin man said.

"Gilbert sleeps where I sleep."

"Then you sleep in the barn with the other animals."

"Gilbert is a free man, as was his father before him."\

"Makes no anyway; he sleeps in the barn."

"Then we both do, until I find another place. It looks like we're here for a few days."

"You don't find nobody in this town letting a nigger sleep in a bed inside. They'd have to set fire to it right after he left."

"We'll see about that."

Henry did not send anyone immediately to replace Elliott and his men. He thought it would be a good lesson for his son.

Indeed it did prove valuable, because for the rest of his life, William did not make an important move without first identifying all the possible results and preparing for them in advance.

The other things he learned were that he enjoyed being a merchant and selling to people, and that Gilbert was worth his weight in many ways.

At the same time, Gilbert discovered many talents he didn't know he had and also how much he needed to learn.

In the brief time together, they had formed a good bond more akin to friendship than to a master-servant relationship.

Indeed, it would prove to be the most intimate friendship either man would have.

William saw he didn't need to tell Gilbert anything twice. The Negro youth did things well and seldom left loose ends, except when something was beyond his experience.

Agnes Barker 1858

The two young men labored for almost two weeks keeping the outpost going.

In the meantime, William also learned a little bit about being a Negro, even in the North.

For two days they slept in the barn, until a stout, amiable woman walked into the emporium and announced she had a room for the men.

"I hear you can't get no room to sleep in nor much good food because of that fella there," she said, pointing to Gilbert.

"Well, I have a spare room just aching to have boys in it agin. And nobody ever complained about my cooking."

William looked at her in surprise and said, "We could surely use some good cooking and a place to sleep that doesn't have straw all over it."

"I live at the end of Oak Street just off the pike. Just follow your nose and the odor of good food when you finish tonight. Those clothes could sure use a washing as well. My Delilah will be happy to wash them for you."

William and Gilbert had outfitted themselves from the store stock but preferred their own clothes whenever possible.

William and Gilbert smiled at each other. Another problem solved.

Agnes Barker walked out of the emporium with a slight smile. Things had been tough for her and Delilah for quite a while. She was mostly shunned by townsfolk and made a living cooking, sewing, and making up to people.

The residents of Greenwich tolerated her but never forgave her for taking in a foundling Negro baby some fool mammy had left on her doorstep.

"Hossasfrats, the joke's on them," she often thought. Delilah was her daughter, sired by a blacksmith's assistant at a time when she was lonely and depressed.

Agnes' father was the village blacksmith, as his father was before him.

Her mother was a preacher's daughter who was taken up with the efforts of northerners to foster the emancipation movement, and their house was a way station on the so-called Underground Railroad for runaway southern slaves headed for Canada.

One of these runaways was a blacksmith, and her father put him to work in the forge rather than have him go north.

He was big and strong, and had a wonderful smile.

Agnes's husband went off one night to find a Kit Carson, who was blazing a trail to Santa Fe, or so he said.

She had never heard from him again and that Negro, Big Jeb, was there one night when she was really lonely.

They played together for four months until slave catchers got wind of his presence and he fled in the night. He too never got in touch with her. After he left, she found out she was pregnant and decided to have the baby in secret.

Her mother helped, but—just days before the baby was born—she died, falling out of her chair from a sudden heart attack.

Her father followed her mother just after the baby was born in secret, either too unhappy or too ashamed, or just lost without his wife.

Agnes staggered to their funerals, leaving the baby alone because she had no one to trust.

The story about finding her on her doorstep was accepted because the townspeople knew about her mother's work with the Underground Railroad.

Forced to sell the forge, she eked out a living for the next fifteen years until William and Gilbert stayed at her house.

William and Gilbert enjoyed their first good meal and sleep in Agnes's house.

Delilah washed their clothes and stared silently at the men during dinner.

She was up ahead of them to give them breakfast but said little during the first two days.

Agnes kept the conversation going, learning much about the two young men.

She never quite trusted William but liked Gilbert.

He in turn opened up to Agnes, and on the third day, he started to notice Delilah.

She was tall, with an ample bosom but a flat bottom, and with strong arms and legs.

Agnes had taught her much of her domestic skills and to read and write.

Delilah's experience in the village school had not been pleasant.

The other kids taunted her about her lack of parents and sometimes about being almost white. For it was a fact that her complexion was very light and smooth, and her hair did not have the usual kinkiness often seen on other Negroes.

Unfortunately for Delilah, the few other Negroes in town resented her light complexion and avoided her when possible.

Agnes was not religious but drove Delilah each Sunday to the Baptist church favored by Negroes in that part of Connecticut. It was Agnes's secret hope that her daughter would find a husband among the young men of the church.

While she was eyed by them, none made the trip to Agnes's door.

In Gilbert, she saw a possible solution to her problem, for Agnes knew she was dying.

The village doctor had said so, but not in so many words. Nonetheless, Agnes knew it in her heart.

For Samuel Gilbert, it was the start of a relationship with the Prescott family that lasted until his death. It would bring a fortune to his family.

Delilah Barker 1858

All her life, Delilah Barker knew she was different. Not only was her skin lighter than other Negroes she had seen, but her hair was also not as crinkly. In other ways she was a stranger. She played with other Negro children at school and church but noted they were not as friendly toward her as they were to other playmates.

Then, too, her mother was a white woman who treated her like a daughter, saying she was left at her doorstep.

By the age of twelve, she knew that was a lie. She caught Agnes Barker looking at her with affection when she thought the child was not aware. They never talked about their relationship, and Delilah did not press the issue.

She knew she was loved and cared for, seeing Agnes quietly giving her more of their sparse meals.

When the two men—boys, really—came to live with them, she saw the meals were a bit bigger than normal.

"They need to eat good," Agnes replied when Delilah asked about the change.

Delilah washed the clothes, seeing the differences between the white boy's clothes and the Negro's clothes when they first came to the house.

Over the two weeks, she saw a change. Within the week, they were dressed in almost identical woolen shirts and trousers.

She mentioned this to Agnes, who had also noted the change.

"The rich boy don't skimp on Gilbert's clothes," she said.

Gilbert had also seen that when choosing clothes, William always picked out two of everything from the emporium stock.

In all his life, Gilbert never had a new pair of anything. It was a strange feeling, and he was grateful.

The boys worked long hours in the store and were happy when one of the men sheepishly came into the emporium and asked for his job back.

"I don't know why you let Elliott go, but I need work," he said.

"If you come to spy, I will fire you if I find out."

"I need the work."

"Then come back, and if I like what I see, I will tell my father."

At night the two boys walked the town, talking to those people who would draw near. The town gossips were intrigued by the events, but William said nothing. The townspeople were also curious about his refusal to sleep apart from his companion.

When they started to live with the Barker mother and "foundling," there was more to talk about.

William's manner, inherited and learned from his father, won many people over, and by Friday, no one was boycotting the emporium, despite Elliott's best efforts to get customers to stay away.

Their first Saturday in town was also the time for an annual picnic. The four people at the Barker residence attended, with William supplying a barrel of cider.

"Its goodwill," he explained to Gilbert, who didn't know the word.

William saw to it that they had a good place under a tree for the picnic. Some townsfolk came by to greet him and Agnes but paid no attention to the two Negros. William said nothing but kept the memory.

Gilbert and Delilah were left to themselves and talked about their upbringing. Gilbert told tales of growing up in a large family while Delilah listened enviously.

Toward evening, they strode to the banks of the nearby river. Gilbert was getting use to and enjoying to the new clothes he wore and hesitated before putting his coat down for Delilah to sit. He sat on the grass and immediately noted the stain on the pants seat.

"Now, I'll need to wash that tomorrow so you can wear it on Monday," she said.

"I've got another pair," he said, not telling her that it was the first time in his life he had two of anything.

"How long will you stay?"

"I have no idea. We sent a message to Mr. Henry, but he hasn't replied."

"We sure like your company."

"Your mother's a good cook."

"I cook half the meals."

"Really? When we get to your house the food's ready, so we thought it was Miss Agnes who cooks."

"Sometimes, when she's feeling poorly, I cook."

"What's wrong with her?"

"I don't know, but sometimes it's hard for her to get out of bed."

"How did you come to live with her?"

"The story is she found me on the doorstep."

"Like Moses in the bulrushes."

"Something like that."

"You don't believe that?"

"No."

"What do you believe?"

For the first time in her life, Delilah told someone she believed Agnes was her mother.

Gilbert was surprised by her admission and didn't know what to say.

"Now, don't go and tell anyone, especially that other boy; he'll think me uppity."

"It's our secret."

"You'll be leaving soon."

"I hope so; I miss my family."

"I wish I had a family."

"You got family—Miss Agnes."

""But I don't know what I will do if anything happens to her."

Almost without thinking, Gilbert said, "If that happens, you come to our house, and we'll find something for you."

Both Delilah and Gilbert were shocked by the statement.

Neither said anything but looked at the river, Gilbert awed by what he had said, and Delilah gushing with gratitude.

"You can kiss me if you like. I ain't ever been kissed."

For his part, Gilbert had never kissed a girl as well. There was an awkward, pregnant pause as they looked away from each other. Gathering up his courage, he leaned over and kissed the waiting girl. It was not a good kiss, but it thrilled them both. Gilbert ventured another kiss, and she responded, pushing her face into his lips with a fervor she didn't know she had.

They lingered by the river until called by Agnes, who smiled as the two walked back to her.

"They've been spooning, just as I hoped."

Throughout the following week, Delilah and Gilbert grabbed quick kisses when they thought no one was looking. Their ardor was so intense that even William finally caught on.

"What are your intentions about that girl Delilah?" he asked one day when they were alone in the store.

"I dunno, but she's pretty and smart and can cook."

"Good reason to spark such a girl, but it's a long way from our home."

"I guess so," was all Gilbert could reply.

The next weekend William was invited to the home of the village's richest man. The invitation was specific to include only him, and he was about to decline when Gilbert said he would like to borrow a rig and see some of the countryside. William did not ask if Delilah would accompany him but was smart enough to know she would.

The young couple went out to the fields surrounding the town with a picnic lunch, a first for both of them. They lay on a blanket and kissed ardently, but for some reason Gilbert did not try to undress her. She had made up her mind to let him if he tried but said nothing when he held back. Both were frustrated, unhappy, and a little sad as they got up to return.

They came home to find Agnes in bed and ailing.

Delilah cooked a light supper, and the two sat on the porch. Both were afraid of the future and said little.

"I don't know how long I'll be staying," he said.

"You'll leave and forget me."

"I don't think so."

"You don't think so?" she said angrily.

"No, I never met a woman like you."

"You're just eighteen; how many women have you met?"

"I mean no one has made me feel like this before."

"Like a man who wants a woman," she said.

"You can have me if you want."

"I don't just want you that way."

"Ain't no other way."

"Yes there is," he replied quietly.

The rest of the weekend saw much tension in the household, with Delilah and Gilbert seething with emotion, and Agnes so ill that the doctor was called.

Events moved quickly as William's father finally succumbed to Rebecca's pleadings and sent a new manager and crew to relieve the two men.

They arrived one Monday morning along with Henry.

He stepped through the emporium doors with a tight smile on his face and went straight to the ledgers in the office.

He examined them first, William standing silently by, not saying a word.

Closing the ledgers, Henry looked up at his son and said, "Well done."

He never said another word about the incident but was secretly pleased. He knew then that his son would carry on the company.

Both men took their leave of the Barkers, Agnes noting that Gilbert lingered long in saying goodbye to Delilah.

William noticed as well.

"What are you going to do about that girl?" he asked on the way back.

"I dunno, but if I can, I will marry her."

"I think she would have let you have your way with her if you tried."

"I know that, but I want more."

"You're young and should saw some oats before settling down."

"A gal like her is enough for me."

William liked what he heard and decided he had found the man he could trust.

William Prescott 1859

After his adventure in Connecticut, Henry was pleased with his William and gave him more and more responsibilities within Prescotts. He went with his father on trips to their emporiums and on buying missions throughout the East.

Father and son developed a style of working together that suited each. Often, Henry would allow William to negotiate a purchase, swallowing hard when his son was outfoxed by more experienced traders. Afterward, he would tell his son what he did wrong, but he honored the agreements.

Gilbert was often along on these journeys or was put to doing tasks to expand his knowledge as well. Some men snickered at the Negro boy but quickly learned he had an agile mind and never made the same mistake twice.

Both Prescotts liked what they saw in the young man and trusted him more and more during this period.

They gave him time off to see Delilah as she nursed Agnes during her final illness.

Once, in New York City when the Prescotts were alone, the father took the son to a high-class bordello.

"It's time you became a man," was Henry's only comment.

William found the experience unrewarding and unsatisfying.

His next experience was hurried but much more fun in the closet of a New York merchant's house, with the merchant's daughter.

She was ugly but ardent, and their lovemaking was quick and again unsatisfying.

William fell in love for the first time with a neighborhood girl who broke his heart.

Francine Harding grew up five houses down from his home and was a natural-born flirt.

She was blond, petite, and sensuous, having experienced sex at fourteen, and she enjoyed having boys fight over her affections.

William intrigued her, and she contrived to encounter him one day as he left the house.

"You're the Prescott son, aren't you?" she said to him boldly.

"That I am," he said carefully.

"Is it true you're half-Jewish?"

"Yes."

"My father says you're smart, but I think you're handsome as well."

William said nothing to the girl in front him, thinking how brazen she was.

"Why don't you come to my afternoon meeting time this Saturday?"

"I don't know if we finish dinner in time."

"Oh, yes, the famous Prescott dinners. I think my father resents not being invited all these years."

"What does he do?"

"Why, he runs a bank just like your mother."

"My mother only advises the bank."

"That's not what people say. They say she runs the bank that your family stole from banker Cashman, and he committed suicide."

William became a little angry at the story floated by Cashman's family.

"I think people have the story wrong, but that's not my worry, it's theirs."

"You're very sure of yourself."

"I know what happened."

"Do you?"

William smiled for the first time at this young lady, noting her eyes were blue like his father's.

"Perhaps we can meet Saturday night?"

"I have some boys coming over afterward. Come then."

"I think not. I'm not good with crowds, and I would want you all to myself."

"My father doesn't like it when I am alone with a boy."

"He would like it less if you were alone with a man. Do you dare?"

She turned her head away from him and smiled.

"I could meet you later down the street, and we could walk along the bluff."

"No, I will meet you at your house after the boys leave."

"My father would not like that."

"It is that or nothing," he said, sure she would not refuse.

Harold Harding looked on in disgust as his daughter left the house with William that night.

"He's a Jew," he said to his wife.

"Only half so and very rich," his wife, Samantha, said.

"I'll not have Jewish blood in this family."

"I don't think Francine is going to marry him."

"It's about time she started thinking of marriage. She's eighteen, with a whole gaggle of boys hanging around her."

Francine said nothing, knowing the Prescott boy was already pulling his weight with the family business.

Their first walk was more a sparring contest, with each being careful to show no emotion except one of indifference.

At the time, a bluff of rolling hills wove through the Oranges, separating sections of inhabitants. The bluff looked out over little farms and clusters of houses, each grouping usually centered on a family or ethnic group.

As night fell, they made their way back to her home.

At the door, she turned to him and put her cheek up to be kissed.

"When I kiss you for the first time, it will be on the lips," he said.

Surprised, she lifted up her skirt and went inside. Closing the door behind her she smiled. "Another admirer to be tamed."

Into the fall their walks continued, and she smiled when her father was invited to a Saturday supper.

"Damned if I'll go," he huffed.

"Don't curse in the house, and you will go. I've been dying to see their house and to join that group," his wife said.

"Besides, this Saturday our rector will be there; we can't disappoint him, can we?"

She didn't dare point out Francine was invited as well. Her father was surprised when she joined them for the short walk to the Prescotts. He was even more surprised when she was seated next to the son, William.

"I'll not have a Jew in the family," he whispered to his wife, surveying the table that included some of Rebecca's relatives.

For her part, Rebecca eyed Francine closely, sensing her son may have marriage on his mind.

Francine met her gaze with a cool look, casually resting her hand on William's wrist, s

eemingly saying, "He is mine if I want him."

Rebecca understood the gesture and decided then and there the girl would not have her son.

Her mother saw the gesture and inwardly recoiled. She knew her daughter, and she knew her husband. If Francine wanted William, her husband would forbid it.

Henry remained oblivious to everything that was going on as he pumped a visiting congressman about the coming election.

"There is danger in the land," the congressman was saying.

"I fear for it as well, Congressman," he replied abstractly.

"There will be war if the southern states go through with their threat to secede."

"I hate war," Henry replied, having escaped from service in the Mexican-American War but profiting handsomely by supplying New Jersey volunteers during that conflict.

Right now, he was weighing what to do if war did come.

Not particularly interested in politics but always keen for more profits, he had been approached by some men who wanted to buy clothing manufacturing companies.

"A war is coming, and the army and navy are going to need clothing, and we want to be able to supply them at a good price," was their mantra.

Up until that time, Henry was primarily a middleman to other retailers and to his customers. Investing in these mills would be a major change, and he was beginning to not like change.

At fifty-five, he was beginning to tire of the grind and yearned for William to shoulder more and more of the company leadership.

When first broached with the mill idea, William was enthusiastic and urged his father to participate. In fact, William thought they should do the project on their own, but Henry cautioned patience.

"We need to learn the water's depth before we jump into the creek," was Henry analogy.

At dinner's end William and Francine walked onto the porch.

Rebecca contrived to take her mother into the front parlor.

"Our children seem to be hitting it off," Rebecca said.

"They have been seeing more and more of each other," was the reply.

"Do you think that is good for them?"

"No, I think not," was the short reply.

"Then we are in agreement."

"Oh, I do agree. I will speak with my daughter."

"Then I need not talk to my son," Rebecca smiled.

The next day Francine's mother spoke with her when they were alone.

"What are you doing with the Gilbert boy?"

"I intend to make him fall in love with me."

"Do you intend to marry him?"

"No, he is a passing thing."

"Then I need say no more."

However, Francine could not quite give up William. Of the men and boys paying her court, he was by far the most interesting and the wealthiest.

Wealth meant a great deal to Francine. Her father, who owned a toolmaking factory, was well off but not rich. Francine wanted to be rich. She might have seriously considered William as a husband but for the fact that he was half-Jewish.

"I cannot imagine myself having a Jewish man's thing inside me," she had thought when weighing William as a husband.

Still, until she was sure of which man to marry, she kept seeing William. He was by far the most interesting suitor, and the fact that he was half-Jewish both attracted and repelled her.

With each passing week, William became more entranced with his neighbor girl. As fall turned into winter into spring, he saw more and more of her. When he was away, he wrote ardent letters to her filled with hopes for the future. She never replied and in fact wrote only four letters in her entire life.

The Hardings became regular guests at the Saturday suppers, and the father even broached the idea of a business deal to Henry. After careful thought, and at Rebecca's urging, he turned it down, a slight Harding did not forget.

While seeing William, Francine also accepted courting from two other swains, one in particular drawing her eye.

William knew of the other suitors but was unaware of their esteem in Francine's eyes.

He confided to Gilbert his love for Francine but not to his parents. Through her own sources and ways, Rebecca kept abreast of the affair, knowing the outcome would not be good for William.

On her twentieth birthday, Francine's mother took her aside again and asked her plans.

"To marry Elijah Roote."

"Why him?"

"Because after William, he's the richest of my suitors."

"Is that how you choose your marriage partner?"

"Didn't you?"

"No, I chose your father because he was the kindest man I knew."

"Father?"

"Yes, whether you know it or not, he is very kind and generous and loyal. I knew he would never stray from me, and he hasn't."

"He is a bully and a tyrant, but I love him."

"He is afraid for you."

"He need not worry. I will marry safe and rich. And as for William Prescott, I will break his heart—b

ecause they snubbed us all those years and refused to go into business with Father."

"I won't tell your father until after you're married."

Henry and William decided to invest in the mills, and in early August, William went off to Manchester, New Hampshire, to work in a mill and study how these factories operated.

While he was gone, Francine's parents announced her engagement to Roote. Rebecca did not tell her son until he returned late in October.

William rushed to Francine's house, but she refused to see him. He was distraught and did nothing for two weeks but mope around the house. Finally, Rebecca sat him down for a talk.

"She was not for you," Rebecca said.

"But I loved her."

"You will find someone else who will be more compatible with you."

"She was beautiful."

"But stupid and vain."

"I do not need a smart wife like you are to father."

"Yes, you do. You are heir to a great enterprise, and you will need help ruling that enterprise."

"Right now I don't know what I want."

"Yes, you do. When you were born I hoped you would not be your father's son, but you are.

If anything, I think you will be greater than your father, and to do that you need the right kind of wife. Be patient; she will come along—perhaps not this year or next, but sometime. When you do find her, be like your father and seize the moment."

The talk did little to immediately heal William, but events unfolded that put marriage and love out of his mind.

Once Henry and William saw the profits in owning the manufacturing of goods rather than trading them, they decided to devote some of their energies to other endeavors.

Their next investment was an iron mining and smelting company in New Jersey. The owners needed capital to expand as war preparations expanded. They turned to the Prescotts, who advanced them the money with the option to buy.

Again William, this time accompanied by Gilbert, went to work in the operations, where the hard work with hot furnaces hardened their bodies.

While Henry was less enthusiastic, William was excited by the prospects offered in the evolving American industrial expansion.

Further expansion for Prescotts would have to wait.

With the election of Abraham Lincoln, events moved quickly to the firing on Fort Sumter in South Carolina and the call for volunteers.

William received a lieutenant's commission in the 1st New Jersey Zouaves. Gilbert was his orderly, with the rank of sergeant.

For Gilbert, a life-changing event occurred when they finished a three-month training period.

With her mother just dead, Delilah showed up at his home the week they were to leave with the regiment.

Never having mentioned Delilah to anyone in his family, her arrival was a surprise.

Gilbert embraced her and asked for help in having her stay in East Orange until they returned.

William arranged for her to stay with Beatrice's family and to become a maid in the Prescott's house.

Delilah was not happy as a maid in the Prescott house but stuck grimly by until Gilbert's return.

Gilbert and Delilah were married six months after the Battle of Chantilly (Ox Hill). William was the best man. Beatrice stood up for Delilah.

Their first son, named William, was born a year later. Their second son was named Abraham, after the younger Prescott.

Two daughters and another son would die without issue, something the Gilberts mourned deeply and secretly.

Abraham would serve the Prescott family, but in a very different way.

Rebecca Prescott 1860

The president of the Orange Central Bank was uncomfortable. He sat in his office and stared at Rebecca Prescott as she reviewed the monthly ledgers. Caleb Huntington had spent all his life at the Orange Central Bank. He rose from assistant teller to president by dint of hard work and attention to detail.

When Amos Cashman lost control of the bank during the financial crisis and Rebecca became more involved, Huntington saw an opportunity and seized it to ingratiate himself with the new owners.

His reward after five years was the bank president's position, which he had held ever since.

Today he was worried because of this unannounced visit by Mrs. Prescott. Her monthly review was not due for another week, yet she arrived minutes ago and asked to see the ledgers. That they were accurate and up to date was not the problem. But why was she here?

"You may be wondering why I am here, Amos," she started off the conversation.

"Always a pleasure to have you come in."

"Don't give me that guff, Amos, you like running this bank by yourself."

He didn't respond to the truthful statement.

"I'm here because we have decisions to make."

"About what?"

"We're not getting any younger, and we need to look to the future."

Again, silence from the banker.

"Whom do you have to replace yourself?"

It was a question Amos had thought about himself. Because he never felt secure in his position, he had discouraged the hiring of bright young men and deliberately kept much of the operations in his hands. As a result, his staff was loyal but mediocre.

"Ahem, I have not given that much thought."

"I have, and it bothers me."

"I don't expect to retire soon."

"Well, I intend to stop looking over your shoulder."

"That would be the bank's loss."

"But it would make you happy."

Again, he didn't respond to the truthful statement.

"Before I do, I want to make sure the bank has a future. Right now, you are the bank, and while it is good for the moment, it won't be in the future. What are you now? Sixty-two?"

He jumped in. "Sixty-one."

"The world's changing, and we need to change with it."

"I have delivered profits and growth."

"And done very well doing it."

"Thank you."

"No, I mean for yourself, but you've left the bank vulnerable, should anything happen to you."

"We have a capable staff."

"As long as you're around to direct them."

He said nothing.

"There is not a person on the staff right now who could step in, should anything happen to you. You've hired people who don't have the brains to run this bank, just to keep it going."

"I haven't seen the need."

"Well, I have, and we need to do something about it."

"I'll find someone, if that is what you want."

"I have found someone, and I want you to train him to succeed you within two years."

"I hadn't planned to retire."

"I'm planning for you. We'll give you a good pension, but I want to make sure the bank has someone capable to replace you."

Huntington was stunned by what she had just said. His wife and he had no surviving children, and his position was what governed his life. He did not mention the lucrative deals he was privy to as bank president, and the nice nest egg he had built up by investing along with some of the bank's bigger depositors.

"Who is this person you want me to train?"

"His name is Daniel Archibald, and I have hired him to start Monday as assistant cashier."

"What is his background?"

"He has worked for Prescotts since he was fourteen, and we are quite pleased with him."

"Then he knows nothing about banking."

"Precisely; that is why you are going to train him."

"But is two years enough time to take over for me?"

"I think so. Banking is not hard if you are careful. Prescotts is run in the same manner as you do the bank—careful attention to details and cash. We don't do anything without being sure of the results. You have done a good job of keeping our losses from loans down and representing the bank. Archibald has proven himself to us, and we think he is the man to replace you."

Huntington was stunned by what she was saying, and a tide of anger rose within him. Being the good banker he was, he continued to say nothing.

"You can see I am right about this."

"I would need to think about what you are saying."

"You don't need to think about it. It is happening. To make this decision easier for you, I am going to stop coming here and looking over your shoulder. For the next two years, you can run the bank without me."

With this Archibald here in her place, he thought.

"Come now, Caleb, think of this as a retirement present. You have a chance to be free of me and Prescotts."

"I will think about it."

"Nothing to think about. Archibald starts Monday, and this is my last visit with you."

She got up and left the office, leaving a saddened man behind.

Archibald walked into the bank that Monday and remained for almost forty years, gradually assuming more and more responsibilities within Prescotts.

Rebecca's decision—for she had laid out the plan to Henry only when she was about to institute it—was to have far-reaching consequences for the company.

When the Civil War came, and America's economy exploded, Prescotts was in a position to grow with the country.

Ironically, it was William who saw the potential, and thanks to his mother's foresight, he had the tools in place to follow his dreams.

The conversation in the bank was also a liberating moment for Rebecca, because her life too was changing.

William Prescott 1861

The splatter of blood hit A. William Prescott's right trouser leg as he turned to look at General Philip A. Kearny. He saw the man fall off his horse and gasp on the ground but had little time to react as rebel infantry poured fire at the three other horsemen who followed their leader into Confederate lines.

It was September 1, 1862, and the battle of Chantilly (Ox Hill) was coming to a close. This dirty little indecisive battle had just cost the Union one of its best-prepared and most competent generals.

William had no time to think but rode back to what he thought were the Union lines with Minié balls passing him in his flight. One ball hit his horse and another bit deep into his left leg. The pain was sharp, and blood began to pour down into his boot.

Another ball hit his horse, which jumped, almost throwing him to the ground.

He held onto the pommel and kicked the animal viciously.

The horse responded by going faster when another missile knocked William's hat off.

On his right, Major Ebenezer Closter was hit by two balls simultaneously and fell from his horse.

The staff sergeant to his left lost the general's flag as he too was hit. The flag and pole fell onto William's horse, causing him to go even faster.

The two men made it into a copse of trees just as another barrage of shots hit the leaves and trees around them.

It was then that William fell from his horse and lain stunned and bleeding on the ground.

Voices shouted at him to stay down as still a third barrage hit the woods.

The voices sounded familiar, and he was conscious enough to realize they came from his men of his New Jersey regiment.

All of sudden, the roar of howitzers blasted away, deafening everything around him.

It was the Franklin Division artillery hammering the rebel position.

A man in the distinctive red uniform of his brigade bent over him.

"Stay down, Major, this isn't over yet."

William stayed where he was, recognizing the pain in his left leg.

I wonder if I will lose it, he thought.

William stayed where he was for another hour or more. He never knew how long he was in that copse, for he suddenly passed out from loss of blood.

When he woke up, he was on a wagon jostling him to God knew where.

There was a rude tourniquet around the leg wound, but blood still seeped out.

He fainted again.

When he woke, a man in a bloodstained white apron was looking at his wound.

"You've lost a lot of blood, and your bone is shattered," the man said to him.

"Please don't take it," William managed to blurt out as he grimaced in pain.

"I doubt you'll ever walk on it again," the man replied.

"Don't do it," William said again through the pain.

"Gangrene can happen if I don't."

"Pour some liquor over it, put on a bandage, and take care of the others," William said in his most commanding voice.

"You'll die if I don't."

"Send for my orderly, Sergeant Sam Gilbert."

"I don't have time to do that; we have these other wounded men."

"Just get Sergeant Gilbert and leave me alone."

The man shrugged, said something to an orderly, and did as William asked. The pain was doubled as the doctored poured the liquor over the wound and left.

William passed out again, awakening only when Sergeant Gilbert poured some brandy from a silver flask into his mouth.

"Get me home, Sam," was all William said before passing out again.

William never knew how and in what fashion Sergeant Gilbert managed to get him from Fairfax County, Virginia, home to East

Orange, New Jersey. Nor did he learn how the man got permission and transportation all in four days.

All William knew was awakening in his own bed with a small, wizened man looking at his leg and clucking quietly.

His mother, Rebecca, was behind him, and his father stood at the bottom of the bed.

"William, you had to go to war," his father, Henry, said. His father never used his first name, and his mother had long given up getting him to respond to Abraham.

Rebecca had insisted on the name for a dead grandfather, as was the custom of her people. The son accepted Henry's desire to use the name William. It was the only issue he ever saw his parents continue to bicker about.

"I could have kept you out of the war. But you had to go fight," his father continued.

His mother shushed him quiet while the doctor continued to examine the leg.

"You will never walk properly again," he said.

Dr. Abraham Strauss was Rebecca's cousin, twice removed. He had a thriving medical practice among the Jewish community in Newark and its immediate suburbs. It thrived because he was the best doctor in the area.

Occasionally, when Christian doctors were baffled by an illness or could not determine a course of treatment, they would bring him in to consult, but normally only Henry's family used him on a regular basis.

Sergeant Gilbert stood quietly in the background.

Dr. Strauss worked on William's leg for more than two hours. He then encased it in some plaster of paris after first splinting the leg.

Each time he moved the leg, William wanted to scream but didn't. His parents looked on but said nothing.

William finally fainted again, with sweat beading his forehead.

For three months, Dr. Strauss worked on his leg, which gradually responded to these ministrations.

William did not lose his leg, but it withered, and only after another two months was he able to walk with the help of cane. The cane would remain with him his whole life and was buried with him when he finally passed away in 1903.

Throughout his convalescence, Sergeant Gilbert was at his side. First, the quiet orderly took to carrying him when he went to the bathroom or downstairs for part of the day.

It was not until the spring of 1963 that William found himself well enough to talk with his father about the future.

"What do you do now?" his father asked.

"I have an idea on how to make money. Lots of money."

"I thought you'd come into the business with me," his father said quietly.

"Oh, I intend to, but not as a junior partner and not to just run a group of stores."

"What do you intend to do?"

"There is a lot of money to be made in this war, and I intend to make it."

"How can we make more than we're making now?"

William proceeded to tell his father his plan. Simply put, William intended to outfit a group of sutler's wagons and follow the troops.

"These soldiers need a lot of things that they don't get from the army," William said.

"There are a lot of people following the Union armies all over the country. They rob, they cheat, and they take advantage of the troops. I intend to offer fair prices for the supplies I offer and buy things that soldiers everywhere pick up," he went on, excited by his audacious scheme.

His father looked at him sternly.

"You can barely walk and you want to go back to war!"

"I have had enough of fighting. I can't tell you how scared I was after General Kearny was shot. I don't intend to have that happen again. But I have seen how there is much money to be made. With your connections, I can get as many sutler licenses as I want. We go into business and help the Union while making a fortune for us."

William and his father discussed his plans over the next few weeks. In the meantime, William asked for and got his discharge from the army, arranging for Sergeant Gilbert to be released as well.

William laughed on finding out he had been given a brevet promotion to colonel and had even been put up for a medal. Putting on his uniform for the last time, he went to Washington to receive his medal. He laughed harder when the medal was pinned on his tunic and he was invited to meet President Abraham Lincoln.

A little embarrassed by the medal, he spent the time in his private moment with the great leader revealing to him the fact that his first name was also Abraham.

William brought Sergeant Gilbert with him to the White House, eliciting stares from the crowd of onlookers who every day stood outside its grounds.

With his medal on his uniform, William then made the rounds of army commissary officials, gaining their respect and, more importantly, the licenses he wanted.

William and Gilbert joined the Army of the Potomac on June 12, 1863, while it was encamped just south of Washington, DC.

As a former officer, William was welcomed by Major General Joseph "Fighting Joe" Hooker, the Army of the Potomac's commander. He received a less cordial reception from General George Meade.

The latter did not particularly like sutlers; he felt William should be back in uniform and not following the army, providing goods and services and getting rich from the troops.

It was here that he began to use his brevet title of colonel. It was ironic to him but gave him stature with other officers. In time, he came to enjoy being addressed in this fashion.

The first day that the two men set up shop, they were approached by a woman in fine but tattered clothes.

"Do you need help?" she asked.

"We're all right here," William replied.

"You're new here and don't know the rules. Big Ox runs the sutlers, and he assigns girls and a place to each wagon."

"Not this wagon and not you," William said.

"You don't understand; those are the rules."

"Have Big Ox come see me," William said.

"No, you go see him."

"Tell him to see me."

She walked off in a huff and spat at them as she left.

William reached under the wagon seat and pulled a revolver from its holster. Gilbert did the same from the back.

An hour later a group of men approached William's wagon. A giant of man, six and half feet tall, weighing more than 250 pounds, and in a faded blue army uniform with sergeant stripes, approached the wagon.

"I understand you don't know the rules."

"I have a license and the right to be here. Outside of that, there are no rules."

"There's army rules, and there's my rules, and everybody follows them," he bellowed back.

"I don't."

"We'll see," Big Ox bellowed louder and strode towards William.

The former major drew his pistol and fired at Big Ox four times, hitting him twice.

Big Ox staggered back, clutched his belly and screamed.

The crowd surged forward.

Gilbert drew his gun and fired once in the air.

The crowd stopped and watched as Big Ox slowly sank to the ground.

The blood pumped from his body, and he began to whimper.

A provost guard detachment hurried up.

The sergeant in charge looked at William, looked at Big Ox, spat, and walked away.

William looked at the crowd and spoke in a loud voice.

"Any more rules I should know about?" he yelled.

The crowd moved back, and the woman who had come to them earlier rushed out to claw his face.

William butted her with his gun, and she moaned as she sank to the ground.

"Anyone interested in helping that fellow?"

The crowd murmured and edged further away. William turned to a group of soldiers from I Corps and said in a quiet voice,

"I am Colonel William Prescott, and these are my wagons. From them you will get an honest deal from me and any other wagon you see with the name 'Prescott.' My father has run an honest group of stores for years, and he sent me here to give you an honest deal. What's more, if you have any goods you want to sell, come see me or my people. We will pay top dollar."

From then on, soldiers quickly learned the Prescott name on a wagon meant fair treatment and no rigged scales.

When the war ended, Prescotts was a name soldiers remembered when they needed to buy or sell anything.

With more than fifty wagons operating throughout the country, Prescott's sutlers were welcomed in almost every army camp.

The following year, William, sensing a real opportunity, had taken some of his wagons to Atlanta and followed General William T. Sherman march through Georgia. That move added more than a million dollars to the company coffers from the buying and selling of "liberated" items taken from Georgia plantations.

Henry Prescott 1865

While his son was away and despite his desire to continue managing the company in his old ways, change was being forced on Henry Prescott. Until the war, he had managed the growth of the Prescott business with a conservative approach. However, supplying the vast demands of Union troops for food and other supplies, the company grew beyond his imagination.

He had banked the profits but found it more and more difficult to find fruitful, safe investments. War bonds, bank bonds, and foreign trading efforts had all proved safe but relatively unrewarding.

At the same time, competition had grown up around him, and he was working longer hours to maintain the company's position.

He admitted to his wife that he was tired and longed for his son's return.

"He may come back with new ideas," Rebecca said.

"I hope so; I'm too set in my ways, and I don't know if they'll keep us growing in this new world."

"Is he making money for you now?"

"Quite a bit."

"Give him his head. If he makes mistakes, we'll still have the business."

"I don't know how much longer this will work."

"You've trained him well."

"Too well, judging by how his sutler's business is doing."

The two parents waited for their son's return with hope and a sense of uncertainty.

They both keenly felt the absence of their son.

Rebecca shared in many of her husband's business affairs. But as the company grew, she primarily reserved her advice for when they were alone together.

Henry and Rebecca still remained each other's most intimate companion.

Their lovemaking continued and was one of contentment and mutual love. She was content with her life, mourning only her lost children.

He never begrudged her anything, and the house ran well under her guiding hand. Rebecca never learned to cook, but a succession of Negro cooks kept him well fed and contented.

With more time on her hands, she visited her parents on a regular basis and had good if distant relations with her two sisters and two brothers.

Her ties to family were tenuous. William and she were invited to family events, but she often went alone.

When growing up, her son had little interest in meeting or interacting with her family.

To her regret, he was baptized rather than have a bar mitzvah, even though by Jewish law he was a Jew through his mother.

Her siblings ran the family business in Newark alongside their father until the older man's death, and the four children nursed their mother through her final illness.

She even sat shiva with them. Henry came each night to pick her up but except for an initial call did little else.

As she grew older, the tug of her background became stronger, but her love for Henry kept her locked into their relationship.

Their son was educated as a Christian, and she said nothing.

Through the years, their lovemaking was one of tenderness and knowledge of each other.

Once a sister asked her if she was happy. Her reply was simple: "Yes."

William Prescott 1865

In Washington, William watched the final march-by of the Army of the Potomac and Sherman's western-theater men for two days, then headed north with Gilbert by his side.

When he arrived home, William sat down with his father to review the last three years.

Both men were satisfied—William with his effort and the money he had made, and Henry with the knowledge that the family affairs would prosper in the next generation.

Henry drew on his pipe and spoke quietly to his son.

"What do we do next?"

"We open a bank, father," the son replied.

"We already own one bank, and we have good relations with a number of banks; why go into competition with them?"

"Because there's a lot of money not being banked. If we can get monies from people who are not using the other banks, we can do a lot more things."

"What group is that?"

"From two sources—the Christian people we already trade with, and from the Jewish

merchants you deal with on a day-to-day basis."

"I can see our current customers dealing with us, but those Jews bank with each other,

and through New York Jew banks when they have something bigger."

"Yes. For their long-term savings and bigger deals. But we're here in New Jersey. We're in Connecticut. We're in Pennsylvania, Ohio, and Indiana. It takes time for these people and other merchants to get money, and sometimes they need it quickly. As I traveled through the South, I realized that in some towns, there was sometimes a Jewish moneylender or pawnbroker who acted as a sort of bank. But they only dealt with part of the town and with each other. Over time, if they came to trust us, we could have a steady supply of capital and savings to invest. More importantly, they could feed us new clients. People are inventing things all the time, and they need capital to grow. We're in an age of change. Just look what the war has wrought. New cannons, new guns, new ways of supplying food. Railroads, highways. Everything is changing. With changes come opportunities, particularly for those with money and a willingness to risk it on new inventions or ways of doing things."

Henry looked at his son, not a little frightened.

The Prescott fortune was based on incremental expansion and growth. His son was putting out a vision he had not even glimpsed.

"And how do you propose to get these Jews to open their pocketbooks and give you their money?"

"Father, whether you like it or not, I'm half-Jewish. Mother's family is well known, and we have built a reputation for honesty over the years. Why not trade on it?"

Thus was born the Merchant Bank empire.

The first thing William did was change the name of their one bank to the Merchant Bank of New Jersey. The next step was to found the Merchant Bank of Connecticut. A Merchant Bank was founded in Indiana and Ohio within two years.

The controlling stock was owned by Henry and William jointly, and William oversaw all aspects of the operations. He built the banks on very conservative terms, starting them in little, out-of-way towns near cities with a large pool of merchants and farmers and enclaves of Jewish families.

Getting people to trust his bank was easier because of his efforts during the war. Every town had at least one veteran from the army, and his sutler's reputation helped build trust.

To break into the Jewish network, William relied on current Jewish customers to pass the word to other communities about his banks.

To further his efforts, he learned Jewish rituals, beliefs, and mores, relying first on his reluctant but pleased mother but then gaining additional insight as his dealings widened. He went about hiring young Jews to staff at least one position in each bank. He was careful to have a distinguished Christian citizen lead the bank. To identify them, he fell back on the numerous contacts he had from his Army and sutler days.

There was one other source of learning, his wife Sarah.

William Prescott 1866

It wasn't by accident William decided to open his next bank in the same town where Gilbert and he fired the manager of the Prescott emporium. In the time he was there, he got to know the people not only in town but also in the surrounding farms.

Prescotts was known there, and the local bank had closed in the intervening years.

He also knew the man who would run it, Silas Whittaker. He was a farmer's son who had risen to Captain in the 21st Connecticut Infantry. Gilbert and he had run into him while following the Army of The Potomac.

"The Colonel," as William Jr. like to call himself when doing business, was impressed with the man. Gilbert went with him when he journeyed to the little town on the Avon River.

Silas was surprised to see them as they drove up to the farm owned by his father.

"Good to see you, Colonel," Silas shouted from the front yard.

Like many Connecticut farms of this era, it was prosperous and well maintained. Good farming land was scarce in the state and keeping the lands together as the generations unfolded was difficult. There were three sons in the family, and all worked the farm. Silas was the second son, and unless his older brother died, he had little chance of inheriting the farm.

Unlike many men who went to join the armies during the Civil War, he wanted to remain in the area of his birth.

Silas was intelligent and had risen from private to captain because of his natural leadership qualities. He had even been encouraged to remain in the army after the war ended.

Silas thought about it. Thought about his prospects. But most of all he thought of Amy Goodman, his childhood sweetheart. He refused the commission and came home.

Amy was there waiting, but his prospects were not good.

The Colonel jumped from the wagon and smiled at Silas. He saw a tall, heavyset man with large hands and a deceptively open smile.

"Good to see you, Silas."

"What brings you to our town?"

"Actually, you."

"Me?"

'Yes, I'd like to talk to you about something we're doing."

"Let's sit in the shade of the porch."

Gilbert jumped down on the other side of the wagon and joined the two men on the porch.

"We're opening a bank," the Colonel said without preamble.

"A bank?"

"Yes, right here in your town."

"We haven't had one since Caleb Summers died, and our bank closed."

"I know. But more and more, people are going to need a bank."

"Hell, we've been going twenty miles to do our banking. Most folks just keep it in a barrel or crate in their homes."

"Banks are going to be needed more and more, and Prescotts is going to open them in towns like this."

"Well, if there are soldiers in those towns who remember your sutler wagons, they'll likely bank with you."

"I'm counting on that."

"Why are you telling me this?"

"Because I want you to run the bank here."

"Me?"

"Yes, I saw how you handled your men during the war. They respected you."

"Wasn't hard; I knew most of them. They came from these parts."

"I know, but it was how you handled the new men that came in from different places as the casualties mounted that impressed me."

"Just treat them with respect, explain what they have to do, and do it with them."

"Many officers say that; you did it."

"If you say so."

"Silas, you're the man I want here leading the bank we open."

"I don't know anything about banking."

"But you know people. To be successful, a bank's got to lend money. Lending money is easy, but knowing who to lend to is the hard part. You know how to judge people and how to treat them."

"If you say so."

"I say so, and that's why I'm here. You won't inherit this farm, so what do you want to do?"

"Been thinking about it."

"This is a way for you to stay here, avoid having to leave, and do your neighbors a favor. I intend to run our banks like we ran our sutler's wagons, honestly and fairly."

"Some bankers haven't done that."

"I know, and it's going to get worse. You know how we treated the soldiers fairly. Well, we will treat our customers just as fairly."

"Sounds like a good idea, but why me?"

"I intend to put local men in charge of our banks and let them run those banks."

"What if I fail?"

"Then Prescotts loses its money, and you come back to this farm."

"How do I learn to be a banker?"

"We'll teach you."

"Who's 'we'?"

"Gilbert and me."

"You know that much about banking?"

"Actually, probably not as much as we will in a few months. You see, you're going to be our second bank. We'll learn by trial and error what we don't already know, and what we learn here, we'll use in our next banks."

"'If I leave the farm, they'll never take me back."

"Do you really want to farm the rest of your life?"

Silas thought a moment and looked at his future.

"I guess not."

"We'll start you at $400 a year and a bonus of 10 percent of any profit."

"I don't know if Amy and I could live on that."

"You're married."

"Want to be as soon as possible."

"Then I'll give you a $200 personal loan to set up housekeeping if you join us."

"Why me?"

"Like I said, you know people and how to treat them. What's more, you're honest and respected. Banking is built on trust."

"How long will you stay with me here?"

"I think two weeks before you open and the first week after you open. Thereafter, we'll be around every month to look at the books and help you figure out problems."

"How do we communicate?"

"By sealed letter every week and by telegram if there is an emergency."

"I'll have to think about it."

"I'm here two or three days to clear out a space for you in our emporium. I figure we can hold down expenses in the first year, but the manager will need to start looking for a separate building.

"Do you think you can get a charter?"

"Been to Hartford and filed all the paperwork. Took the liberty of putting your name as the president. They think a lot of you up there."

"Pretty sure of yourself."

"No, I put Gilbert's name on there too."

"What's Gilbert got to do with this?"

"He'll be your boss. He will be my main contact with all the banks we start."

Silas looked at Gilbert, who stared back because this was the first he had heard about the arrangement.

They left Silas's farm and drove back to town.

"Wonder if we will need to sleep in the stables again?" The Colonel mused.

"Some things don't change," Gilbert said.

"We'll see soon enough."

"What did you mean about me being his boss?"

"Just what I said. You're a father now, and you've been with me a long time. Hell, you saved my life and my leg. My father and I have had some talks about how things should be done. I'm going to be going all over the country setting up these banks, getting all the paperwork, and seeing people. Somebody has got to stay in East Orange and make sure everything is being done properly. One thing I have learned is where there's money there's fraud. Not everyone we hire will be like Silas back there."

"Some men won't like having to report to a Negro."

"Damn right they won't like it. One of the reasons I chose Silas was because I saw how he treated Negro troops. He fixates on the task to be done, not the color of the skin of the people doing the job."

"That's a big responsibility you're asking.

Why do you think I can do it?"

"Because you and I have been doing it for years, and you're darn good at it."

"I dunno."

"Yes, you do. Here's my proposition. I will give you $5,000 when we get back to East Orange, and you can go and do anything you want. Or, you can stay with me at a good salary, and when I die, you get 2 percent of Prescotts. That way, you know you're building something for your family."

"You're buying my loyalty?"

"I have that already; I'm just telling you what I will do for you."

"Why not now?"

"Because let's face it, if it became known you own part of the company, there would be a lot of complications. But mostly because I want to run the company my way. My father has already more or less agreed, and for my lifetime, I want complete charge. If I'm successful, we will build a great enterprise."

"So $5,000 now or some big payoff when you die?"

"That's what I'm offering you."

"How do I know you will do what you say?"

"Because you have my word on it."

"Then I guess the answer is yes."

"Good, now let's find out if we're sleeping in the stables."

Silas became the first president of the Merchant Bank of Connecticut and remained with the company until he died in his office chair in 1890.

His son and two grandsons worked for Prescotts into the twentieth century.

The same landlord who refused them rooms on the first visit gave them a room during this visit and each subsequent journey.

He added three dollars to the bill after each visit because he burned the mattress they slept on.

Ironically, he was the first customer of the new bank. He also took out the third mortgage the bank made to add an addition. The building is still an inn, but now caters to families and travelers looking for a quaint New England hostel.

William Prescott 1869

At the same time he started his first bank in 1866, William, or "The Colonel," as he liked to be called, began looking around for his first investment. He was also looking for a wife.

For this, he turned to his mother. She had grown somewhat stout in her later years and at the same time somewhat melancholy. This sadness came from the realization that she had grown too far away from her childhood roots. She had taken to attending services at the local synagogue and joining other older Jewish ladies for teas and other events.

Mother and son had long discussions on the type of woman who could help him.

William favored a woman with little or no education who could bear him children.

His mother thought otherwise.

It was at one of the gatherings for women that she met Ruth Rellin. The woman was known in the community as the matchmaker.

Whether by design or not, Rebecca casually mentioned to Ruth her son's desire to marry.

Rellin leaped at the remark but kept her lips tight.

"He is half-Jewish, isn't he?"

"But knows nothing about us. About our traditions. He is not even circumcised."

"For a man, that is not a problem. For the woman he marries, perhaps."

Ruth allowed a month to go by, during which she learned as much as possible about William before arranging to encounter Rebecca again in the Strasser house.

The Strassers were musicians, he on the violin, she on the piano. They had built a reputation in musical circles, and he had even been invited to play at the new Metropolitan Opera House.

Isaac Strasser met Irene Gutterman in Germany at a concert where he was the soloist and she was asked to accompany him. They discovered a unique ability to communicate musically. She never learned he was a homosexual who spent a lifetime hiding that fact from family and friends.

They were married six months after meeting and moved to the United States at his urging. Hidden from her was the knowledge that he was fleeing a dangerous, all-consuming affair with a Prussian military officer.

Their only daughter was born shortly after arriving in America, and they named her Sarah.

From an early age, unlike her mother, Sarah sensed there was something odd and hidden in her father's life. She loved both her parents and wondered why there were no more children after her.

Irene never spoke about those things, and Sarah only asked once. The answer Irene gave further baffled her: "Because that is how Isaac wants it."

Sarah was musically inclined but preferred books and science to being proficient on an instrument. However, she was a very good pianist. But she had early on decided she wanted to be a doctor, and to further that goal, she threw herself into science studies.

There were few ways a woman could become a doctor in the 1860s. One was to apprentice with a doctor who was willing to face the scorn of fellow practitioners and tutor a woman.

Another was to go to one of the few colleges willing to accept women as students.

Sarah also faced parental objections, but as usual in such cases won her point, and in 1863 she went off to the Woman's Medical College of Pennsylvania. Founded by Quakers, it had relocated adjacent to the Pennsylvania Women's Hospital by the time she enrolled. It lasted as a separate institution until 2003 before being absorbed by Drexel University Medical University.

Sarah loved her time at the college and earned her degree in 1865. Coming home to East Orange, she struggled to get her practice off the ground. She was reduced, in her eyes, to serving only women patients but yearned to have a fully rounded practice.

Sarah had another problem. Few eligible men courted her.

Her profession put off a lot of young men who desired her for her beauty, for she was one of the most beautiful women in New Jersey.

Her breasts were firm, almost voluptuous. Her face was oval, with eyes that looked out at the world in an open, inquiring way. They were blue and clear, a throwback from an early ancestor, for neither parent was blue-eyed. Her legs were long, and when she looked in a mirror, she saw a reflection much better than those of her women friends, of which she had few.

Sarah had a decisive nature and made decisions quickly and with confidence. A childhood scar reached from her left eye to her hairline, and when she was angry, with a patient, friend, or suitor, it grew redder. Because of her training and working with nurses and doctors who treated women from all walks of life, she was not afraid of sex. In fact, she looked forward to having sex with a virile man. In her mind, the act was a natural outgrowth of human existence.

Sarah thought often of a prostitute she treated, while still a medical student, who was having a baby she was putting up for adoption.

As the contractions increased, the woman did not scream but rather talked about her customers, often by name.

"They're all there for one thing and don't give a damn about you. So it's up to you to think about the things you like, and if you like what he's doing, lie back and enjoy it."

The woman was dead two weeks later from the lying-in sickness, and the baby died shortly thereafter.

Sarah sometimes thought of her and looked forward to her first time with a man.

In the meantime, she suffered the few suitors who came by or were brought by Ruth Rellin.

She was nice to them, but no one had raised any feelings in her. Certainly, none gave her the urge to go to bed with them.

Ruth shrewdly thought there were few men to satisfy the woman doctor but kept her counsel.

When Rebecca mentioned her son, something sparked in Ruth's brain.

After learning more about William and deliberately meeting him one day, Ruth knew she had found the right man for Sarah. Now it was up to her to make things happen.

She was happy. After all, isn't this what God had made her for?

In April 1866, the tenth, to be precise, Ruth called Sarah from her office in the house to meet Rebecca.

Bothe women looked at the female doctor and stifled a gasp. Sarah was dressed in an old dress over which she had placed a doctor's apron. Her hair was unruly, as she had just cautioned an obese, pregnant patient about the complications to be expected in the birth of her ninth child. Sarah did not expect her to survive the delivery and feared for the baby.

"This is Sarah Strasser, and she is a doctor," Ruth said.

"It is good to meet you. You are a credit to us," Rebecca managed to say.

"My pleasure as well," Sarah said. She examined Rebecca with a doctor's eyes and saw oncoming sickness.

"Do you eat a lot of starches?" Sarah asked.

"What do you mean?" Rebecca replied.

"You are gaining too much weight for your bone structure. This puts a strain on your heart and knees. It also hurts your lungs and other vital organs. Women who are too fat face more problems than those who are not."

Ruth blanched, but Rebecca sensed a warming feeling for this woman.

She tried to smile away the words and turned to Ruth.

"What an unusual woman. I must ask Doctor Strauss what he thinks about what she says."

Ruth murmured some quiet words and asked Sarah, "How does the practice go? Are you getting patients?"

Sarah sighed and said she was getting some but believed she was too frank with the women about their conditions.

I'm not surprised, Ruth thought.

Later in the week, Rebecca sent Sarah an invitation to dine that Saturday at her home.

Early in their marriage, in a concession to Rebecca, Henry agreed to having Saturday dinner at two o'clock. This coincided with many Jewish residents coming home from synagogue. The arrangement proved advantageous to Henry's business, and the practice had become an East Orange ritual that lasted until Rebecca's death in 1875.

Interestingly, neighbors seldom attended these open dinners, but other businessmen and their wives were frequent guests.

That Saturday, William met Sarah for the first time. He was scheduled to go to Indiana the following day.

He felt an immediate attraction to Sarah and tried to hide his walk and leg from her.

"You've had a serious accident, haven't you?" she said to him at the table, Rebecca seating them next to each other seemingly by accident.

"It's actually a war wound. But it is nothing," he replied.

"The recovery must be because of Dr. Strauss," she said. "He is the only one I know who could save legs and arms. We have so much to learn about treating wounds."

"Yes, it was," William said, with more force than he wanted to display.

"It must hurt when you walk for a long time."

"Sometimes even a short walk will pain me."

"Then let's just walk to the porch after we eat."

Rebecca watched the two young people out of the corner of her eye. Henry, who knew his wife well, followed her eye.

Another Jew in the family, he thought.

Sarah and William walked to the porch and sat in adjoining chairs. They talked for an hour, but neither could ever remember what they said.

She left after six that night and wondered if he would do something more to see her.

William cursed himself for not telling her he was leaving for a month to open the bank in Indiana.

William often thought of Sarah during the next five weeks.

She too thought of William.

Rebecca, through Ruth, discreetly let Sarah know William was away.

He returned on the Fourth of July, only to find out that Sarah had gone to Philadelphia to join classmates and others in the celebrations.

Philadelphia has always been a center of celebrations for the nation's birthday, and this year was no exception.

Veterans of the still-recent Civil War were marching for the first time in units, and there were celebrations all over town.

Hearing she had gone to the Quaker City, William on impulse went there too.

As a veteran with an obvious war wound, he found no dearth of people willing to help him find Sarah.

He finally caught up with her in Independence Park, where she was with a group of doctors and nurses.

"Why did you come to Philadelphia?" She asked hoping for the right answer.

"To see you!"

"You could have waited till I returned to East Orange."

"I could not wait a day. I've been thinking about you since we met."

"So have I."

They looked at each other, and he grabbed her hand.

"Come with me!"

She followed him out of the park and down the street to the Claridge Hotel, just opened in time for the occasion. Her heart missed a beat when he walked boldly up to the registration clerk.

"I want a room for tonight and possibly tomorrow."

The clerk looked at him, then Sarah, saw there was no luggage, and was about to say they were filled when a $10 gold piece hit the desktop.

"We have a cancellation," he smoothly said, as he pocketed the coin.

"We'll take it—and arrange to have supper sent up," he said, as another gold coin plopped down on the wood.

"We don't serve dinner for another two hours," the clerk said, grabbing the second double eagle.

"That gives us enough time. Keep whatever is left over from the second coin."

Sarah was flustered, bewildered, and scared, but she followed William up the stairs to a quiet room in the back. It wasn't the hotel's best, but it did for them.

They were married less than a month later.

The young couple followed both parents' wishes by having Jewish and Episcopal ceremonies on successive days.

Ruth attended both and during the second ceremony quietly slipped the envelope Rebecca gave her into her large handbag.

She thought she had done God's work again.

By the time his son, William Jr., was born, the banks were thriving, and William was deep in investing in some of the new inventions appearing during the 1870s and 1880s.

Sarah Strasser Prescott 1870

Like many couples, Sarah and William got to know each other better after they were married.

William assumed Sarah would give up her doctoring and keep house for him.

She thought William understood her desire to keep helping people, especially women.

It also heightened their disagreement about where to live.

Again, William assumed they would move into the big house in East Orange.

Sarah wanted a home of her own.

Her father even offered to build one on a lot he had purchased just down the street from the Prescott residence.

Like many couples, they compromised.

They moved into the Prescott house, and William reluctantly assented to her continuing her practice.

When she said she was pregnant, William was elated, but she felt a loss she couldn't quite acknowledge.

William the second was born eight months after the wedding, to much clucking about the premature birth of an eight-pound boy.

A friend from Pennsylvania Medical College for Women delivered the boy amid much joy.

Henry was pleased with a grandson. Rebecca was happy the boy was Jewish, as heritage is passed down through the mother. Sarah's parents were ecstatic until they were apprised that he would be baptized at the Grace Episcopal Church.

Glumly they attended the ceremony, as did Ruth Rellin.

Another envelope from Rebecca eased her conscience but not her fears.

How will he know our faith, raised amongst the gentiles? she moaned to herself.

With the baby at her side, Sarah continued to see patients in a room off the main entrance.

She noticed some patients, especially the poor and those of questionable trades, were reluctant to come to the big house.

Part of the problem was solved when a women's clinic was started by wives of East Orange's more prominent citizens. She found out later that William had become aware of the situation and acted to help his wife.

"It gets them and her out of the house," he said to Gilbert.

With slight encouragement from William, Sarah left the baby in charge of Delilah and the other household help.

With her gone, William took an active and strong interest in the boy.

By the time his sister, Rebecca, joined the household, the two Williams—father and son—had become close.

Blind to many things, like his father was, William never noticed some things that were different about his son.

William Prescott 1873

The previous year, Sarah thought it would be good for their children to visit Europe.

She wanted to go as a family. Her wishes coincided with William's own thoughts.

They went to Europe with Gilbert, Delilah, and their sons and daughters.

While in Europe, William secured a working arrangement with Jay Cooke and Company.

William agreed to sell the English bank's bonds to his depositors, relying on the British firm to examine and back the offerings.

Just one year later, Jay Cooke failed, one of the major causes of the Panic of 1873.

William was caught with a large position in worthless bonds and a severe lack of cash.

He was forced to close some of the depots, downsize others, and tighten credit lending at the banks, and he saw his own personal fortune considerably reduced.

The Prescott fortune did not revive until 1881.

For the next five years, Henry and William worked long hours shoring up the family banks and other investments.

They paid off every dollar lost by clients in the Jay Cooke disaster. For this, they won the gratitude of those clients and built up the reputation of William's banks. This effort paid dividends in the years to come. The loyalty of these customers and clients drove the expansion of the banks as well as the distribution company.

This single act, combined with his efforts as a sutler, established the reputation of Prescotts as an honest company.

Through the years, this company's commitment to fair dealings was tested by insiders and others.

In the end, its reputation for honesty and integrity would prove to be one of its most enduring strengths. At the same time, the family's blindness to the foibles and greed of employees almost destroyed it.

Through referrals from clients and customers, Prescotts came to invest in many new invention and services springing up in the country.

In time, fully a third of the Colonel's time was devoted to managing this side of the business.

Despite the demands and trials of his business, the Colonel knew his company would survive, prosper, and grow.

More and more as time passed, Henry deferred to his son. He became somewhat melancholy after his wife's death.

William, now called "the Colonel" or "Colonel" by everyone, also knew he would need a strong heir to carry on after his death.

That heir would be William Jr., and to his training the Colonel spent many hours in thought and actions.

He also began the habit of finding capable people to help him run Prescotts.

He started with Gilbert, who became and remained his most trusted advisor until almost his death.

When potential associates bristled at being managed by a Negro, they were immediately let go or never hired.

Gilbert was rewarded very well, the Colonel even arranging for a house to be built at the edge of the Negro section of East Orange.

It would remain a Gilbert family holding into the twentieth century.

Though ambivalent about Negro issues, the Colonel and his descendants remained sympathetic to their plight.

Rebecca Zimmerman Prescott 1875

When she gave up control of the Orange bank, Rebecca began the slow process of divorcing herself from the everyday happenings of Prescotts.

She remained her husband's confidant, but the loss of William's two siblings depressed her.

So too did the continued estrangement from her family.

By 1869 both her father and mother had died.

Her brothers' businesses were prospering, and their sons were following in their footsteps.

For the most part she attended family gatherings alone, with Henry coming along at times, but she saw there was a gulf that appeared never to be bridged.

When Sarah Strasser married her son, the gulf grew larger with his insistence they wed in the Episcopal Church as she had done.

Sarah's father and mother attended, but no one else in her family came. It hurt her.

Her two sisters, happy in their households and strong in faith, were more friendly, but still there was a sense of estrangement.

Sarah proved to be a good daughter-in-law, sharing with Rebecca some of her own estrangement.

While not particularly religious, Sarah shared many private thoughts with Rebecca. They tacitly agreed about the sacrifices they had made to marry the men they loved.

Henry and she were still close, and her love for him never wavered or diminished.

As the years passed, her body filled out, but he still sought her in their bedroom with the same ardor.

William gave her much satisfaction, but he was caught up in affairs as the company grew even beyond her dreams.

He sought her advice much as his father did, but more and more she saw he was his own man.

"Like father, like son," she thought one day late in 1870 when she realized Henry was slowly being supplanted by his son as leader of Prescotts.

Henry was devoting much of his time to looking at new things while William took over the day-to-day running of the company.

"I like it this way," Henry said to her one night as they nestled in each other's arms.

"Because you have more time for me?"

"That too, but I think he his building something you and I only dreamed about."

"Are you happy about that?"

"I think so."

"You have a grandson who will carry on after William."

"That pleases me but more; it will give William a reason to grow the business."

"You did not need a son to do that."

"No, I had my father to spur me on. And you."

"Do you remember those walks when we talked about the future?"

"I often do. It was a scary time for me."

"Why?"

"Because I was telling you my secrets and my fears, and I didn't know what I would have done if you did not marry me."

"I was scared too."

"Of what?"

"Of you not marrying me."

"Well, here we are all these years later, alone in our bed with a great company at our feet."

"I would have continued to love you if you had failed."

"I could not live with myself if I had failed."

"You didn't, and you haven't."

"We have been through a lot, and I worry every day that we will lose everything."

"If we did, we would start over and be successful."

"You really think so?"

"Oh yes. You would find something else and build anew."

"Not at my age."

"At any age."

While Prescotts would not fail, the company did have some precarious moments through the Panic of 1876, but Rebecca's steadying influence and Henry's conservative ways pulled it through.

Over the years, Rebecca gradually drew closer again to her Jewish roots.

Ironically, it was the cousin at whose bar mitzvah she met Henry who helped her.

Isaac Cohen was by this time chief rabbi at Temple Beth El, the oldest synagogue in Newark.

"I want to get back," she told him.

"To what?"

"I do not know, but I feel a loss."

"A loss of what?"

"My family. What I was?"

"Do you not love your husband? Children?"

"More than ever do I love the man I married."

"Then what have you lost?

Do you miss your religion?"

"No, I miss the comfort of my family. And who I am."

"You are what you are, but if that is not enough, you must discover what is missing."

"It is my religion I miss."

"Then come back to us."

"It is not easy after all these years."

"Nothing worthwhile is easy."

From that conversation in the fall of 1870, Rebecca became a regular attendee at Saturday services. She still presided over her Saturday dinners but more and more had relatives and Jewish visitors.

Henry saw what was happening and said nothing.

Their relationship changed somewhat with her away with her family in Newark more and more as the decade progressed.

For Rebecca, returning to familiar childhood haunts and embracing her religion again gave her comfort.

Her son also saw the change but said nothing.

Rebecca felt tired throughout the winter of 1874–1875. She consulted Sarah and then a now-aged Dr. Strauss.

Both doctors agreed and talked with her quietly,

"We both agree this is serious and wish we had a cure for you, but we don't," Dr. Strauss said.

"What do I do?"

He shrugged and put his hand on her shoulder.

"It is up to God now; I can do nothing but ease the pain."

Sarah began to cry, abandoning all professional restraint, for she had come to truly love her mother-in-law.

In bed that night, Rebecca broke the news to Henry.

He jumped up and cried out.

"This can't be true. Are you sure?"

"Dr. Strauss and Sarah agree that there is little they can do."

He grabbed her and held her tightly, crying for the first time in his adult life.

They held each other the entire night and in the morning began the last journey of her life.

The illness progressed, and as spring came, Rebecca was almost totally bedridden.

Rabbi Cohen came often, Henry leaving the room when he appeared.

The husband abandoned all interest in his business while his wife lay dying.

William was heartsick for his mother, realizing what an important part she had played in his life.

The end came as May turned to June.

On her deathbed, Rebecca reviewed her life and found it on the whole very nice.

What girl gets the man she dreamed about and finds him to be truly the man of her dreams? she thought.

Her final vision was of Henry's tear-stained face.

Henry allowed for a Jewish funeral at Temple Beth El and even sat shiva with the family, as he knew that was Rebecca's wish.

He buried her in a family plot near his home and visited her every Saturday that he was at home until his own death.

William Prescott 1885

Prescotts was a growing enterprise when William decided to move his business out of the house and to a new office building on Main Street. There were simply too many people working with him, keeping track of the Prescotts enterprises. Gilbert was his number-one advisor and in fact ran the day-to-day operations.

Some of the white men working in the office resented him. They didn't last long, but some of those who stayed were fathers and grandfathers of future Prescotts employees.

William's choice of the building wasn't by chance. He didn't bother to tell people he owned the building but pretended he rented the second-floor suite.

Gilbert also broke precedent by hiring two women to clerk and type.

One of his choices he regretted.

One of the reasons William moved out of the house had to do with a female typist hired the previous year to operate the newly popular Remington typewriter machine.

Approaching his fiftieth birthday, William began to see his mortality.

His father was nearing eighty and still involved in the business.

Except for prostitutes while young, William had never known any woman but Sarah and thought he was satisfied.

When Gilbert suggested getting a typewriter to speed work, William was noncommittal.

Mary Blume was hired by Gilbert and was not seen by William until she reported for work the first day.

When that day arrived, something snapped inside William. While they worked at home together, William did nothing. His ardor for Sarah cooled, and he thought of nothing else at times but Mary.

She for her part was aware of William's interest, as was Gilbert. He wanted to fire Mary, but something told him to leave the situation alone. Gilbert did contrive as much as possible to be in the same room when they were together.

Once ensconced in the Main Street office, William saw to it there was a large sofa in his office and a large bathroom with bathing facilities.

Gilbert knew what was happening but said nothing, not even to Delilah.

The inevitable liaison began in the fall of 1885 and continued on a regular basis through the winter of 1886.

Mary Blume was the daughter of a drunkard Jewish watchmaker and an Irish Catholic girl from Newark's North Ward.

Seeing how dependent her mother was on her wayward husband's irregular pay envelopes, Mary vowed at an early age to be dependent on no one.

When she was fourteen, she lost her virginity to an Irish relative of her mother.

At fifteen, she was a regular "pump house" for Irish boys in the neighborhood.

With her grammar school education finished, Mary looked around for a trade she could depend on.

Her last teacher told her about something new called a typewriter. She took a horse trolley down to a demonstration at the Newark Trade School.

Overcoming any inhibitions, she asked the demonstrator if she could try the machine.

After watching him, she put her fingers where he did and typed out a sentence.

Seeing Mary's figure and aptitude, he offered to teach her.

She suffered his advances for four weeks and saw her speed increase to fifty-one words a minute with almost no errors.

One Friday she kicked her teacher in the balls, then interviewed with Gilbert on Saturday morning, and started work on Monday.

Within months she was William's paramour and figuring how to turn this to her advantage.

Mary had no illusions that the arrangement would last forever and wondered what she could get out of it.

The answer came when she missed her period. She waited until William had exhausted himself on the couch.

"I have something to tell you," she said.

"Not now; let's enjoy this moment."

"It can't wait."

"Everything can wait."

"We don't have much time."

"My father doesn't expect me until three."

"He'll have to wait."

"I see; I guess the moment has passed anyway."

"I'm having your baby," she said in a matter-of-fact way, not portraying her own feelings.

William jumped up and pulled on his pants before asking, "Are you sure?"

"I am sure, and I know it's yours."

William began pacing the floor.

"Oh, oh, oh. I can't make another baby with Sarah, and you say you're pregnant. I don't believe it. If it's so, maybe it isn't mine."

"Oh, it's yours, Mr. Prescott; there's been no one else for months."

"I'll talk to Dr. Strauss on Monday. He can do something about the baby."

"You forget I'm a Catholic. We don't kill our babies."

"We need to do something, Mary. You can't have that baby."

"It's our baby, Mr. Prescott."

"But it can't be born."

"It will be, and you're the father."

William paced up and down in his office, running through the various implications of this awful news. He faced her again.

"You can't have that baby," he said again, in a sterner voice.

"It's just not done."

Mary sat straighter and looked him in the eye.

"I'm a Catholic, and we don't kill our babies."

William continued to pace his office. His thoughts were of William Jr., and what news of a Catholic half sibling would do.

"How much money will it take to have you go away, have the baby, and not be seen again?"

Mary smiled to herself. The future was looking a little brighter.

"I thought you loved me, Billie boy."

"Scandal is not what I need, nor does the company. How much?"

Mary took a deep breath and said, "Five thousand dollars."

William was shocked.

"Five thousand dollars! That's a fortune."

"I won't kill my baby, and you want me out of your life."

"The trouble is I don't want you out of my life.

"Well, there is no halfway. Will you marry me?"

"I can't leave my family, my mother, my children."

He didn't realize he had neglected to say Sarah.

That day, they settled on $2,500, and they walked out together, not noticing the woman seated in the window of Popagora's restaurant.

Sarah looked at them and wept quietly, her tea growing cold as she watched them go down the street and part at the corner.

James Camaron Prescott 1888

On a spring day in 1888, James Camaron was newly arrived from the Protestant area of Ireland when he walked down the Bowery in New York. He was twenty-two years old and would live almost seventy years from this date.

In that time, he would help build the Prescott fortune to a point little dreamed of by either current leader.

James was not thinking of the future when he entered the pawn shop at the corner of A Street.

He was calculating how much he could get for the gold watch, his last possession; it had belonged to his father, a Belfast doctor who had eventually succumbed to the syphilis he had caught from a street prostitute back in 1850.

James reached America by working as a stoker on a White Star packet. It was an experience he did not ever want to repeat.

At just over six feet, with black hair, wavy black locks, strong, piercing eyes, and an insolent manner that women swooned over but that his father had detested, James was forced to leave Belfast ahead of an angry father and a pregnant minister's daughter he had seduced in the choir loft one Sunday after services.

James wasn't sure the baby was his but thought it prudent to leave.

An obliging stewardess at White Star thought it would be fun to have him on an Atlantic voyage, but stokers and other crew members didn't mix. She was probably disappointed he didn't make the return trip, but one crossing was enough.

New York had not been kind to him.

Jobs were scarce for Irish immigrants in the city, particularly Protestant Irish men.

James was muscular and not afraid of hard work, but he was used to using his brains rather than his hands.

He stevedored for a while, but as shipping activity dwindled, he discovered being Protestant did not sit well with the Irish bosses who controlled the docks.

But being Irish also kept him from many jobs in a city dominated by the white establishment, many of whom were high Episcopal Church.

His boardinghouse landlady was tough, suffered no nonsense, and threw renters out the day they missed paying the weekly toll.

Now he opened the door of the dark cubbyhole that housed the old man who called himself Israel Solomon. James had been there before, slowly dribbling away the few items he possessed from his father. First to go was the medical bag and instruments. This was followed by the old man's cane and watch chain. His cufflinks followed.

James had put them in his carry case during his last visit to the family home.

Their value would have kept the family for a year.

When he stole them, he did not think of his mother or sister.

Nor would he know of their fate until twenty years later.

Solomon looked up from the tiny desk at the man who entered.

"Are you here to redeem your father's bag?" he said with a slight accent. The pawnbroker had come to America in 1860 and soon found himself in the Union army. Six months of hard training and two battles convinced him to leave the I Corps when it camped near Washington. While on guard duty, he simply stepped away into the night and found a synagogue on the outskirts of the city. A kindly rabbi put him in touch with a Jewish community in Fredericksburg, Maryland. From there, he made his way to New York and worked with a peddler, saving every cent until he opened this shop in 1870. He prospered but never married and now sat alone day after day, knowing he would always have a stream of customers.

"No, to show you something else," James replied.

"It is a shame to lose one's family possessions."

"It is a shame to lose one's bed."

"Finding work is hard today."

"It will be harder tomorrow if I am any judge of the news."

"What you need is a trade."

"For that you have to start at an early age."

"It is not too late."

"What would I do?"

"There are new inventions every day. Find something that is new and learn all you can about it."

"Good advice, but how do I eat in the meantime?"

Solomon shrugged.

"So what is it you have for me today?"

"My father's watch," he said as he handed over the big round object.

"So this is your last tie to him."

"Yes, and I don't want to part with it, but the need is too great."

Solomon examined the watch and realized he could get $50 dollars for it uptown at Guggenheim's Emporium. He thought for a minute and let his greed overcome any notion of fairness. He liked James but had long ago learned to put aside any feelings and thought about how the profit would add to his hoard at Manhattan Bank where he and other Jewish merchants kept their profits.

"I will give you $7.50 for it and allow you to buy it back for $10 within a year," he said, knowing he would sell it the following week.

"I was thinking more like $25."

"Too much! Keep it and go down the street."

The two men haggled for an hour, and James walked out with $11. He would return in a six months and find the watch gone from Solomon's shop. He roughed up the old man, and for the remainder of his life he searched for it. James would never find it, and on his deathbed he murmured about a "a gold watch," to the bafflement of the family members gathered to see him die.

James walked past the row of shops lining the narrow cobblestone street.

There were a variety of shops, but the area was rapidly becoming a center for printers.

By 1888, Americans were developing a voracious appetite for printed materials of all types. From books, to pamphlets, to newspapers, to advertisements, to handbills, the printed word, preferably with pictures, was a major source of communication.

As immigrants arrived from various parts of Europe, they also brought with them the ability to read in their native languages. As a result, newspapers and books needed to be set with different alphabets and typefaces.

Printers used a system of individual type hand-placed in forms almost identical to the system invented by Gutenberg in the 1400s. It was painstaking and time-consuming, even for the most adroit human typesetter.

In 1884, Ottmar Mergenthaler of Baltimore invented the linotype machine, which formed whole lines of type. It revolutionized the print industry. In the beginning, Mergenthaler faced opposition from traditional printers, but within twenty years his machine had spread around the world.

At the time James walked the Bowery, there were thirty-four English language newspapers in New York City alone, and more than sixty publications catering to ethnic enclaves ranging from Swedish, to Italian, to Jewish, to one printed in Yugoslavian.

James's way was blocked by a wagon loaded with a strange device. It was a linotype being delivered to a printer,

The owner stood outside as the men put it on the ground. It was too big for the door, and he was moaning as they pulled the front window out of its frame, breaking it in the process.

James looks at the contraption, wondered at its use, and stepped up to the harried man.

"What is that thing?" he asked.

The man ignored him.

He asked again.

The man turned to him and shouted, "It's a linotype machine for typesetting."

The terms were unfamiliar to him.

"What does it do?"

"It sets type."

"Oh," James said.

Throughout the day, James watched as the machine was put into place.

He stood back as the company technicians, two burly men and a better-dressed young dandy, set up the unit.

By this time, there was a crowd of idlers and workers standing around in the shop.

In a shrewd move, the owner was placing the unit in the window so people passing by would see it at work.

By six o'clock, only James and the workmen were left. He had not eaten all day and knew he would miss tonight's meal at the boardinghouse, but still he stayed on as the laborious process continued.

Finally, the men said the machine was ready.

A linotype machine requires molten lead at a certain temperature to form the print line. The temperature must remain at a constant level so that it is not so hot that it melts the surrounding area, and not so cold that it won't flow freely.

The early machines were stoked with coal fired underneath in a chamber about four feet high.

Temperature was controlled by valves letting in the proper amount of air.

The type was created from a keyboard, much like a modern typewriter, but instead of keys hitting paper, the raised letters were formed into a block of type of the desired width.

It was past seven when the young dandy sat down at the keyboard and started to train the man assigned to operate the machine.

The owner, who James now knew was named Otto Stragmeyer, pointed to a man about fifty years old indicating he should sit next to company trainer.

Stragmeyer also pointed to a boy of fifteen to start the fire.

The boy stepped forward, put the coal in place, and gingerly lit the lumps. Because he did not properly arrange them, there was a blowback.

With a shout, the boy jumped back.

Without thinking, James rushed forward, grabbed a poker, and rearranged the coal while damping the airflow valve.

"Get out of there," Stragmeyer shouted.

"Be careful or your floor will burn up," James answered.

The cast-iron retort started to heat, and the lead ingot began to melt.

The company dandy looked at James and smiled.

"You're right! The chamber needs to be constantly watched. Too hot and the lead is too liquid. Too cold and it won't run properly."

"Get in there," Stragmeyer shouted to the boy.

The boy shrugged and started to add coal.

He did it poorly again, and the retort started to get too hot.

James quietly told the boy to take it slow and place the pellets in a circle, overlapping each other.

The dandy kept looking at James as the heat built up.

When he thought it was the right heat, he put more of the lead ingot in, and finally the liquid bubbled and reached the level of the outlet plug to the type form.

He then started typing, and as he did so the lead flowed into the form.

When he finished a line, he stopped, pulled it out, and gave it to Stragmeyer.

It read: "Otto Stragmeyer, Owner of Linotype Machine 100."

Stragmeyer shouted in joy and showed it to the rest of the shop workers.

The type was still warm and his hand hurt slightly, but he was elated.

"Let Gutman see this," he said, referring to his fellow countryman and competitor.

Stragmeyer turned to James and asked how he knew so much about this retort.

James, sensing an opportunity, said he was an experienced stoker, with many years of experience.

"How about you teach my printer's devil here how to do this? I pay you $2 for the rest of the week."

"Well I don't know. I'm due to ship out later this week for a three-week trip to Key West."

"All right, I pay you for two weeks and give you lunch with my family."

James appeared to think about it for a moment or two, then replied: "Make it $2.50, and I will stay home this trip."

"Da! Good! Stay here until we finish today and watch that man and the lead. You started this morning."

All the while, the company dandy eyed James.

"I want to finish the training tonight so I can go home to East Orange. So let's get started."

Until well past midnight the owner, the printer's devil, Elbert Heinemann, the typesetter, and James watch the dandy demonstrate how to use and maintain the linotype machine.

To James, it was a whole new experience, and what surprised him was how quickly he understood how the machine worked—what the critical parts to it were, and most importantly, how to use the keyboard.

When first introduced, the linotype operator used a hunt-and-peck approach to hitting the keys. Modern typing procedures were a few years off, and for a decade or two each operator used the system he devised.

Finally, around midnight the young dandy turned to James and asked if he wanted to try his hand at creating a line.

James jumped at the chance, and to his further surprise, he found he could create a line almost as fast as Heinemann. This brought a grunt from the printer.

It was almost two in the morning when the young dandy left the shop to take a ferry across the Hudson and home.

James went to bed a little later, then woke at dawn to eat a hurried breakfast and be at the shop by 8:00 AM. He thought Stragmeyer was one who expected his people to be on time.

He wasn't wrong, but he realized that Stragmeyer lived in the back, and that the shop ran twenty-four hours a day.

At that time, people expected printed material to be done overnight.

Stragmeyer was well known for delivering on time and with accurate results.

He fired printers who made mistakes but lavished money and care on those who could meet his demanding standards.

In the two weeks James stayed with him, he learned a great deal about the printing business: Its cutthroat ways. How money was made. How it was lost. Which economies added to profits.

But most of all, he learned the ins and outs of the linotype machine. He quickly realized he was faster and more accurate than Heinemann. He also gained a mortal enemy in the older man.

At the end of the two weeks, James was hoping for an offer to stay on, but he realized that Heinemann was working against him.

On the last Saturday—people worked six days a week in those days—Stragmeyer gave him his pay and said he wasn't needed any longer.

A little disappointed, he walked out of the shop.

The company dandy was standing there, dressed for a night on the town.

"I thought they wouldn't keep you. The older guy hates your guts," he said.

James looked at the man.

He stood a little under six feet tall and was slightly built. He looked soft and moved with an easy, almost feminine, grace.

His clothes, James was later to find out, always came from J Press on Fourteenth Street and were custom made.

"It's five o'clock, and I need to be at Delmonico's at six thirty, so let's go to a place I know and talk."

With nothing better to do than to meet a doxy on Ninth Street, James allowed the dandy to steer him north to an enclave of rutted streets intersecting Fourteenth Street.

On Irving Place they passed the house the famed novelist Nathanial Hawthorne occupied till his death and arrived at a ratty tavern called Pete's.

The dandy appeared to be well known in this workingman's hole in the wall, with its loud noise and slovenly women.

Two came up to him at the door, but he waved them away.

"Delmonico's usually doesn't get started until eight or later, but I need to meet my sister there before she goes back to Jersey," he said.

"But in the meantime, let me tell you that I have been thinking about you since we put Stragmeyer's machine in."

James just nodded.

The dandy ordered two bitter-tasting beers and drank part of his before continuing.

"You seemed to catch on about our machine very quickly," he began.

James just nodded again.

"Did you learn the printing business while working at Stragmeyer's?"

Again a nod from James.

"Think you know all there is to know?"

James smiled and said, "I don't think so."

"Neither do I. But I bet you're a fast learner."

"I catch on to things."

"Well, I am planning a little diversion from my current assignment and thought you might be the right person to join me."

"I thought you worked for Mergenthaler?"

"Oh, we have some money in the company, and my father always likes to have someone on the inside learning what makes it go round. I'm here for six months, and then I can tell him where the warts are, and he can be satisfied his money is safe."

"You mean you own the company?

"No, father is one of the investors and holds some prime stock, but he always covers the table when he goes into a fling like this one. He wants to know what may happen and how it can be fixed if things go wrong. In this case there is no question Ottmar will succeed, and when he succeeds, we will be a little richer."

James just sat there in stunned silence.

"Why talk to me?"

"Because I always look for young, intelligent, attractive men to fill in the ranks of our little filabits. Father is always talking about how it's the man that is important, not what the proposal is. He's usually right, so I don't argue with him. In fact, no one except mother argues with him. He's been that way since the Civil War. He was right then, and he's been right ever since."

This latter statement was made in a rather rueful way that James did not fully understand.

Over the years, James realized he'd missed a lot of what was said on that occasion.

The years would improve his perception, but he always doubted if he would even on his dying day have made real sense of what the dandy was really saying.

"Well, enough of this talk. Let me ask you a direct question. Do you know what you're going to do now?"

"No, not a thought. I was hoping Stragmeyer would keep me on."

"Well, I'm glad he didn't, because I have other plans for you."

James sat silently and listened as the dandy went on.

"We are just about finished with Ottmar, and father as usual is seeing beyond the immediate and looking for new fields. And on one of those fields I see you!"

James was a little taken aback but again said nothing.

"So for now, I want you to go to this address on Monday and ask for Sam Gilbert. He will be expecting you. He will give you some books to read and some chores to do. Whatever he asks for in the next two weeks, you do. In the meantime, I will shuck Ottmar and set up a time to meet father. It will be in East Orange, as he almost never leaves the office. I will see you from time to time, and by then we will be ready to discuss what our next field will be."

James sat there, a little stunned and somewhat distrustful.

The dandy must have seen the look on his face.

"I see you are disturbed. Don't be; we will have much frolic. Did I mention you will earn $5 a week for those two weeks? And we only work a half day on Saturday."

Again, all James could do was stay quiet, his mind running on ahead of him.

"Well, this beer certainly doesn't compare with Delmonico's, and I'd best be going there before my sister starts worrying that I won't come at all. I have done that to her in the past, and she always finds a way of getting back at me."

The dandy got up and started to leave. James noticed he hadn't paid for the beers, and that James would be stuck with lading.

But the young dandy said, "Stay as long as you like; I run a lading with these people and pay when father deems to give me my allowance."

James started to rise too but sat down again.

The young dandy rushed out the door without another word.

James sat there a bit stunned.

He finally looked down at the card with the address for Monday written in a small, precise hand. Above it was the name William Prescott, with an address in East Orange, New Jersey.

Sarah Strasser Prescott 1889

After the bitter realization of William's betrayal, Sarah's love turned to hate.

She separated herself more and more from William and the children.

Becky didn't mind, but William Jr. did not understand nor accept.

Sarah spent as many hours as she could away from the East Orange house, even arranging to spend months in Philadelphia as a teacher.

It was during this time that she had an affair with one of the professors, Bruce Siegelman.

During one of her tours at the Pennsylvania Medical College for Women, he noticed her unhappiness. Siegelman thrived on unhappy women. A bachelor, he had arranged his home so women could come discreetly at any hour, and he enjoyed cuckolding other men. A man of renown in his profession and a professed lover of women, he actually hated them.

His mother was unfaithful to his father, and he discovered this fact at the age of fourteen. It was a discovery that warped him for the rest of his life.

Using his usual tactics of professed sympathy and understanding, he aroused in Sarah feelings she did not understand. Nonetheless she found herself in his house, being propelled to the discreetly lighted bedroom.

She had no romantic notions of love, nor did she think of Siegelman as a knight-errant.

What surprised her was the brutal way he took her.

Almost impatiently, he took her clothes off. Approaching fifty, she still had a good figure, and her breasts did not droop.

He grabbed her quickly, laid her on her back, and took her strongly.

His manhood was thrust inside her, causing her to cry out.

He did not mistake this for joy, and thrust even harder.

She began to respond to him as he drove ever deeper into body.

He climaxed before her, just before her own orgasm.

She lay there quivering, not knowing what to say or do.

He remained on top of her, spent with enthusiasm but still not satisfied.

His head on her shoulder, he rested for a five minutes.

The smell of her excited him, and he quickly found himself stirring again.

She sensed his growing manhood and pushed him away, looking into his eyes.

He kissed her hard and moved his hand to her breast. Her nipple, already aroused, grew even more engorged.

Neither said a word as he once more entered her, and she responded with a quick orgasm and a high moan.

Their lovemaking continued until morning, and they slept late.

Twice more they met during her time in Philadelphia.

Each time, he was more brutal, and her vagina ached afterwards.

Sarah had no illusions about him to be shattered, and she gave in to a sensual desire that he satisfied.

She returned to East Orange and took up residence in the house on Elmwood Street, a wiser woman but still angry.

For over a year, Sarah saw Siegelman. Each time, his lovemaking was brutal and strong.

They were naked in his bed when she decided to tell him this was the last time.

"I'm going to stop seeing you."

"What makes you think you will?"

"Because I said."

"No, it is when I say it is so."

"Don't make this hard.

We've had our time. You hurt me each time we meet, and it is time I stop."

"Only when I am ready."

"No this is the last time."

She got up to leave, but he pulled her back, pinning her to the bed.

"When I say it is over, Mrs. Prescott."

"No! No!"

"Yes! Yes!"

He held her down and tried to enter her again. She fought and struggled. He slapped her hard. She lay stunned. He put her hands together and grabbed the sash from his robe. Before she could do anything, he had them tied to the brass bed frame.

She tried to cry out, but his hand covered her mouth.

"Don't scream, or I will hurt you."

She still tried to scream, and he hit her again, this time in the stomach.

"I said don't scream."

She tried to catch her breath. He got off her and found a handkerchief, which he stuffed in her mouth.

Sarah struggled and twisted.

His cock was larger than she had ever seen it. He rammed it into her vagina, causing her great pain. He pounded at her again and again. Her screams died in her throat.

When he was finished, he left her there, stunned and degraded.

He took a class of port from a nearby table and looked at her. His penis was still enlarged.

For ten minutes he just looked at her and smiled.

Putting down the glass, he mounted her again. This time he did it slowly, causing her more pain with each stroke.

Three more times he raped her, each time pausing to drink some port and spend time smiling at her.

With the coming of dawn he stopped, untied her, and said: "Now I say you can go."

She staggered out of the house and went to her apartment. Sarah did not appear at the school for three days, sending word she was sick.

When next she saw Siegelman, he was talking to a student. The sight disgusted her. Somehow she managed to finish the term and go back to East Orange.

By that time she knew she was pregnant.

She poured her heart out to Rellin, by this time a very old woman.

"I know a woman who can help."

"No, it is not the baby I worry about but the shame."

"Men do this all the time, why not women?"

"It is not my way."

"So, what is one transgression against the good you do?"

"I feel so ashamed and lost."

"So, go to the woman I know and rid yourself of his baby."

"It will not erase the horror of that day."

"Over time it will fade, and you will be happy once again."

"I can never be happy again."

"Listen to yourself. What do you tell the women at your clinic? To go on."

"It is not the same."

"Pray, my daughter, and get on with your life."

"I can't pray, and I don't know what to do."

"I will pray for you."

With no one else to talk to, she brooded for two weeks.

On the fifteenth day, she wrote a letter to the head of the Pennsylvania school stating that she would not return for the next term.

The next day she deliberately infected herself from some discarded materials at the clinic and died painfully the following week.

William was inconsolable, as was William Jr.; Becky was stolid in her demeanor and given high praise by all who attended the ceremony.

It was held at the synagogue at her request.

Rellin cried copiously and with great heartfelt sadness.

"What a waste!"

In anger, William withdrew his support for the clinic, but James Camaron Prescott quietly replaced the monies over the years, leading eventually to the foundation of a hospital in the city.

When it opened, the maternity wing was named the Sarah Strasser Prescott Wing.

It was perhaps the best tribute to Sarah besides her family.

James Camaron Prescott 1889

The Prescott banks were thriving as financial institutions and as conduits for financing inventions and new ideas that were springing up. It was generally known that William would take flyers on new inventions.

His banks vetted the individuals, and he interviewed them personally.

One such inventor was Frederick Eugene Ives. Originally from Connecticut, he was a genius and developed the ability to economically take photographs and print them.

Ives and the Colonel met in Philadelphia, encouraged by the Prescott bank president in Ives's hometown.

William's investment in the Morgenthaler machine turned his attention to the printing industry.

He helped to form a company to build Ives's machines for printers and newspapers.

James was sent to oversee the company's efforts in its Bronx, New York, factory.

While helping to expand the usage of Ives's invention, James met a man named Giuseppe Vaiatica.

It came about in a strange way.

As he did with all Prescott investments, the Colonel required someone from his staff to learn all about them.

This time, the task fell to James.

In a Bronx, New York shop where the equipment to create printing plates with pictures was made, a small man came into the office.

He was about forty-five years old and moved with an air of authority, even without a big stature.

James greeted him and asked his business.

"I want to buy one of your machines," the man said.

"Well, we have our regular sales people for that. What publication do you work for?"

"I have my own shop, and I do private printing."

"What kind of printing?

"For discreet gentlemen."

"What do discreet gentlemen print?"

"Discreet material," Vaiatica said, with a slight accent.

Intrigued, James queried the man further, eliciting little more information.

Finally, Vaiatica said he actually wanted to buy four of the machines.

His curiosity aroused, James asked to visit his plant.

Vaiatica hesitated, took the measure of James, and then assented.

"I'm at 45 Prince Street, second floor; come tomorrow."

James agreed and came the next morning.

What he saw was a complete print shop with big printing presses and a group of men working quietly. They all spoke Italian and the one woman, the receptionist/secretary, sat at a desk in the front.

He announced himself and waited until Vaiatica came to the front.

James noticed he said something in Italian and the other men moved to cover what they were working on.

There seem to be a large collection of small books being printed and bound.

As he moved through the plant, he tried to sneak a peek at what they were doing but saw little.

Vaiatica showed him the plant and then took him to what appeared to be his desk in the corner.

"You can see I have a legitimate operation here," the man said.

James nodded and said nothing.

The two men stared at each other for a few minutes.

James finally broke the silence.

"How will you pay for the equipment?"

Vaiatica brought out a big check register and opened it.

"In full, ahead of delivery, provided I can get it by next week."

"All four machines?"

"Yes, just bring them here. I have shops in other cities, but I will worry about getting them to my other shops."

"What about training? It isn't easy to learn how to make those plates."

"Aldo, come here," Vaiatica shouted.

A tall, well-built young man detached himself from a printing press and ran over.

"Aldo will learn and teach the others."

"It takes time, and one of my men will have to be here for about a week."

"I want you to train Aldo."

"That's not my usual job."

"For this order, I insist on you."

James really wanted to know what the "discreet material" was and thought for a moment.

Finally, he quoted the full price for the machines, not mentioning the discount often provided for multiple orders.

"I'll give you that amount today less 20 percent because I'm ordering four."

The two men haggled for about fifteen minutes, finally settling on a 10 percent discount. Both men were satisfied.

James went back to the Bronx a little unsettled and wary.

That Monday, the machines were delivered. James, dressed in workingman's togs, arrived with the machinery.

The first unit was installed that day, and he returned on Tuesday to start the training.

It was not until Friday, when the first plates were produced, that James finally found out what "discreet material" meant.

Vaiatica ran one of the first pornography operations run by the "Black Hand."

Not being a prude and somewhat more "a man of the world" than the Prescott father and son, he did not mention the new customer to them.

James training somehow stretched into two weeks. In that time, he came to like the little man, and Vaiatica in turn came to like and trust the younger trainer.

Seeing James's interest and willingness to accept, and departing from his usual tight-lipped ways, Vaiatica explained how his operation worked. With plants in Cleveland, Washington, and Philadelphia, he distributed what he called "discreet material" to a variety of selling points throughout the Northeast.

These outlets were cigar stores, pool halls, and other gathering places for men. He even had distributors at some of the most exclusive men's clubs in those cities.

On his next to his last day at the shop, James met Angela Vaiatica.

She came into the shop to visit her father, and James was immediately smitten.

Just a little over five feet tall, Angela had both black, dark eyes and long hair. She could not conceal her large breasts or ample figure even in the fashionable dress she wore.

Angela in her turn was taken with the Irishman and smiled tentatively at him.

"Mom needs some money," she said to her father, while looking sideways at his guest.

"Your mother always needs money. I suppose it is for Giuseppe again."

Angela said nothing, keeping her glance on James.

Vaiatica reluctantly introduced his nineteen-year-old daughter to James.

"This is my daughter, Angela," he said reluctantly.

"A pleasure," was all James could muster.

"He's teaching Aldo about creating pictures in print," Vaiatica said.

"Aldo needs a lot of teaching," Angela rejoined.

"He's a good boy, and he will replace me someday," her father said sternly.

"No one can replace you."

"Somebody always replaces somebody."

"But sometimes they are not as good."

James listened to the exchange and wondered if there was something more to the conversation he was not aware of.

Angela strolled over to Aldo, who nearly dropped the plate he was holding.

James did not hear the conversation and only kept looking at the woman.

To James, she was not a girl but rather an object of desire, and his prick started to respond.

He turned away quickly and resumed talking to the father, all the time aware of the woman in the shop.

His interest was not lost on Vaiatica, who proceeded to give him a piercing look while asking him about Aldo's progress.

"He knows what to do, and you're right, he is a fast learner. My job is done here, but I will be back in two weeks to check up on things."

James never did this before and really didn't know why he said it.

Angela did, having heard his last remark. She contrived to stay with Aldo until James was about to leave and followed him out the door ten minutes later.

As she knew he would, he had stayed nearby.

She smiled at him, and he asked where she was going.

"Back home to Grand Street," she said.

"But go up the street and turn the corner; I'm sure my father is watching."

He did as he was told and lingered there until she arrived in the opposite direction, having circled the block.

They talked of little things until reaching Mulberry and Grand.

This was a new area for James, but he spotted a small coffee shop named Ferrara's just east of Mulberry.

He suggested a tea or coffee, and she smiled. "You and I go in there, and my mother and father will know it tonight.

I'll meet you in Washington Square tomorrow at three," she said, and walked away.

James didn't know how he would survive until the next afternoon, wondering if she would show up.

To his delight, she was there before him, talking with two other girls.

They eyed him from head to toe, laughed, and walked away.

"That's Celestine and Francis; they're the only ones I trust, because I know what they do when they leave school.

Angela was a student at NYU, gaining her father's permission to attend college only through a two-year family war.

What really angered her father was that his daughter wanted to go to college, while his son was content to hang out.

Worse, the boy was not even interested in learning either of his father's trades, gangster or printer.

"Let's walk uptown," she said, away from the prying eyes of the close-knit Italian community living south of the Square.

Before either realized it, they reached Thirty-fourth Street.

The couple kept up their clandestine affair for three months before James received a visit from Vaiatica at the Bronx factory the day before he was scheduled to finish his work with the company.

"You're seeing my daughter," Vaiatica said in a quiet voice. "It must stop."

"I want to see her openly," James replied.

"She is not for you or you for her."

"Why not? I'm thinking of asking her to marry me."

"That will never happen."

"If it is what Angela wants, why not?"

"Because she is promised to another, and it is our way."

"This is 1889; the world is changing."

"Not our world and not in this time."

"What will you do to stop us?"

"Kill you," Vaiatica said in an emotionless voice.

James looked at the man and believed him.

Vaiatica was born around 1845 in Castel Del Mare, Sicily. His father had been a member of the bandit group to be known later as the Mafia. Vaiatica at an early age showed that he was not only born into this society but had the wits, brains and ambition to be a leader.

After four successful murders and a demonstrated ability to organize any operation, he was sent to America.

In the Lower Manhattan Italian world, he gained a reputation for viciousness and cunning combined with an almost legendary ability to start illegal operations. More importantly, he knew how to pick men to carry on as he moved up the ladder of the organization. At the time he was speaking to James, he sat on the council of five that met regularly at Paolucci's to plot the schemes bringing money and power to the mob.

His wife, Josephina, was handpicked by Aldo Marazzano to be his helpmate. Unaccountably, after producing a son and daughter, she had suddenly gone barren. No more children issued from the marriage. In truth, she had come to hate her husband and his way of life. Turning to religion and the spoiling of her son, she was a daily communicant at St. Joseph's Church, not receiving communion because she could not confess to Father Joppolo her two abortions.

Undeterred by his wife's refusals, Vaiatica found his pleasure in the receptionist/secretary he had hired when Angela was twelve.

While his son was a disappointment, his daughter both challenged and pleased him.

Now, she was about to be lost, and his anger was white hot.

He looked at James and saw disaster for his family.

"I give you warning, leave her alone, or it will go hard on you."

The older man left a shaken James.

The next day, Angela was sent to Sicily. She managed to get a note to James through Celestine and was away for almost a year.

To prove his point, Vaiatica had two thugs beat up James when he ventured into Little Italy a month later.

The message was not lost on James, and something happened to push Angela from his mind for two years.

William Prescott Jr. 1890

As the man beneath him moaned, William Jr. continued to bugger him.

He drove himself deep into the sailor's ass, grunting in satisfaction as he heard the moans.

"Tell me you like this! Tell me you like this!" He yelled, as the sailor moaned again.

William Jr. was reaching his climax but held off, trying to keep himself at this high level of excitement.

He punched the man's back, hit him on his head, and flagged away with his arms before finally coming.

He stayed on top of the man, still pushing hard against his ass.

Moments passed, and William Jr. was still enjoying the dominant position when the sailor pushed back hard, knocking him off balance.

He never saw the knife as it slashed across his face, cutting a swath across his cheek and nose.

The sailor swung the knife back in the reverse direction, but this time a little lower, cutting William Jr.'s throat and severing his main artery. The blood spurted out, drenching the naked sailor. William Jr. swayed back, toppling over onto his back while grasping his neck.

The sailor laughed as he saw the blood spurt through the fingers.

William Jr. tried to speak but couldn't form words because the knife had cut his vocal cords as well.

He looked up as blood swirled in his eyes. A bright light began to appear in his mind's eye, and suddenly there was nothing. He lay still, the last vistas of thought ebbing.

William Jr. died on the floor of the New York office of Prescotts on a cold December night as 1890 was ending.

He died naked, smeared with semen and blood, and with a horrible, laughing face close to his.

"I hate you dandies, you queers, you faggots," the sailor yelled.

William Jr. did not hear.

The sailor reached for William Jr.'s jacket, took out the billfold, put the money on the sofa along with the dead man's watch, chain, and wedding ring, which he got by cutting off the finger before flinging it onto the sofa.

After washing himself in the little room next to the office, he put on his clothes, stowed the items he had taken into an inner pocket, and prepared to walk out.

He heard a cleaning lady pass by, waited till she had gone to the next floor, and sidled to the stair landing.

The building was only four floors high and had no elevator. He walked quietly down the stairs and out into the almost-deserted street.

A policeman walking by did not take notice. Sailors were a common part of Slip Street, and the nearby taverns and docks were full of them at all times.

The sailor crossed the street and made his way four blocks to his waiting ship.

It was past Governor's Island when Gilbert walked into the office at 9:00 AM.

He saw the open door of William Jr.'s office, and saw him lying there.

It had been thirty years since Gilbert last saw a murder victim on the slopes of Ox Hill. He knew William Jr. was dead. His first thoughts were of the father. It would be a terrible blow to him.

Worse still, it left the company without an heir.

Gilbert closed the door and waited for someone else to arrive.

He was always the first person in the office, even if he did travel the farthest—from East Orange.

The New York office was William Jr.'s idea.

"It will put us closer to the money people and people with ideas we may want to back," he said to his father.

Unstated was the son's desire to get out from under his father's thumb; he had grown almost tyrannical since suffering a heart attack and being confined to his home.

The heart attack had come on suddenly during a Saturday dinner with guests in the house. Fortunately, Dr. Strauss was among them, and his prompt attention was credited with saving William's life.

Hit with the twin infirmities of his leg and heart, the Colonel conducted as much business as possible from the same desk his father had used for many years.

Both still lived under the same roof, although Rebecca had died the previous year and Sarah had accepted a position at the Pennsylvania Women Medical College for the academic year.

That left only Becky in the house with servants and two mentally vital but handicapped men.

James Camaron was the next to arrive at the office.

Gilbert told him briefly what had happened and asked him to go to the police, call back, and get them there.

He next scribbled a short but detailed message to the two men in East Orange and waited for his nephew, the office messenger, to arrive.

Operators were notorious for listening in on conversations. Gilbert wasn't ready to let anything out before the father and grandfather were told.

When he did, he was quickly redirected to take the message.

That left only Benjamin Wasser, the accountant, and Ellie Hampton to worry about. The fortyish spinster came in the door next. Gilbert sat her down at a desk and told her only that William had died.

"Keep everyone out but the police," he told the woman. Having endured much in life, the waspish woman dabbed her eye and went to stand out in front of the door.

A few minutes later he heard Benjamin's deep voice.

"Now, Benjamin," he yelled through the closed door.

The heavyset accountant came and looked for direction from Gilbert.

"I want you to clear all of our papers off the desks and put them in the safe. There'll be a lot of police and others in the offices, and they don't need to know our business," he said, while pushing the accountant to the desk.

With a little help from Gilbert, the desks were cleared within moments.

Gilbert went into William Jr.'s office and checked his desk.

What few papers were there had blood on them, and he decided to leave them alone.

James returned with a fat policeman in tow who took one look at the inner office and immediately went out again.

"Don't touch nothin'," he said when leaving.

The policeman returned, took up a position in front of the murder scene office, and waited. For an hour nothing happen. No one talked.

The silence was broken by the appearance of a man in a well-tailored blue suit and two other policemen.

Detective Thomas Beatty was a first-generation New York City policeman. As a result of his encounter with the Prescotts on this occasion, three generations of Beatty's family would become entangled with or serve the family.

Beatty specialized in murder, particularly when it involved people from the so-called "better element."

He knew to keep his mouth shut when dealing with the upper crust and privileged of the metropolis. He was also adept at figuring out who had committed the crimes. Knowing and proving were different things, especially with rich criminals. But Beatty plugged on, gaining a reputation for solving crimes and knowing when not to press charges.

Sometimes he took justice into his own hands.

He also served Tammany Hall, called by locals "The Wigwam," but at the same time was noted as incorruptible when it came to crime.

He did special errands for people associated with the notorious political ring and was paid in cash for these favors, which had to be within the bounds of his rigid moral code.

As a result, he was able to buy good clothes, eat at nice restaurants, and keep his sister's family well housed in Queens. Three of his nephews would go to Fordham University.

"What's up, O'Toole?" he said to the fat policeman at the door to the office.

"Looks like another sailor killing," was the answer.

Beatty stepped into the office, looked it over carefully, and sighed. He stepped back into the outer office and motioned to James.

"You in charge here?" he asked, addressing the accountant.

Benjamin silently pointed to Gilbert.

Beatty turned and looked at the black man, observed his clothes, and nodded.

"Where can we talk?"

Gilbert pointed to his office, and the two men went inside.

"How did you know the dead guy?"

"I have known him since the day he was born. And his name is William Prescott Jr."

"You know he was a puff guy?"

"Yes, for a long time."

"Know where he met his friends?"

"Not really, and I really didn't try to."

"Well, your bloke in there met the wrong puffer last night. This is the fifth body I've seen with the same cuts. We call him the 'Sailor Killer' because we think he's a sailor, and because of the knife he uses, and the fact we see his work every two or three months. He stays here just long enough for him to kill and hop on a boat to someplace."

Gilbert just listened. His mind was turning over what he would say to Henry and the Colonel.

"Now, we can handle this two ways," Beatty continued. "This looks like a nice, respectable office, and I'm sure you don't want no pack of newspaper hounds mucking in here. If this is like the others we've seen, we're not going to find anything in there to help us find the man who killed here last night. Was the man married?"

"Yes, just five months ago." Gilbert replied.

"Do you want the bride to know what happened here?"

Gilbert was startled by the question because he hadn't even thought of Cynthia Basford Prescott, the society daughter William Jr. had married in Grace Episcopal Church earlier in the year.

"How can we stop her from knowing?" he asked, knowing the answer already.

"Well, I could put it down to an accidental fall and he cut his wrist on broken glass."

There was a long pause, and then he continued.

"Of course I would need to find a way to keep O'Toole and those other two beefs quiet. How much money do you have here, today?"

"Not too much, perhaps $300."

"Well I'll add $200 more, but you'll have to give me $1,000 next week."

Gilbert saw what was happening and made up his mind to follow the policeman's lead.

"I'll get the right coroner to give you the right death certificate. You'll need to give him a hundred when he comes. So here, keep the hundred for him, and I'll do the rest."

The morning and afternoon passed swiftly, as Gilbert arranged for the silence of the burly coroner who came at Beatty's request. He spoke quietly to the other three people in the office.

By the time they thought of lunch, Henry and William had arrived, mercifully after William Jr.'s body had been sent to a local funeral parlor recommended by Beatty, with Gilbert agreeing, not trusting the East Orange funeral parlor to not gossip.

In a closed office, Gilbert told them all that had happened, including the bribes.

William agreed to go to the Park Avenue home that Cynthia and William Jr. shared with her parents to tell her their version of what happened.

Cynthia's father, J. Howard Basford, had an office just off Wall Street, and William went there first.

Basford was called "JH" by everyone. It distinguished him from his father, Howard J. Basford, a self-made millionaire who made a fortune betting with and against the railroad barons, Jay Fiske, Daniel Drew, and their like.

Satisfied with his winnings, HJ retired to his estate on Long Island and left the management of his millions to his son. JH was lazy and in turn left it to his staff, all men who had worked for HJ, to run the office.

Every day, JH exited the office for lunch promptly at noon and commenced drinking his noon-day repast fifteen minutes later. He had a pleasant buzz by 2:00 PM and ate a cold tongue sandwich. He then strolled back to his office to watch activities until the clock struck 5:00 PM.

From his office, he walked uptown to Fourteenth Street and Union Square to his club, the Union League.

From there a trolley ride brought him home at 7:00 PM for dinner with his wife, Lavinia; his son, Howard J, called by everyone J III; and daughter, Cynthia.

Lately, he was often forced to dine with William Prescott Jr., believing the choice was made by his wife's choice for Cynthia's husband. He never realized the decision was really made by Cynthia, over her mother's objections.

JH did not like William Jr., and the feeling was mutual. The older man tolerated his son-in-law because wife and daughter were obviously happy.

William and Gilbert met JH at the door of his office.

"What are you doing here?" JH murmured through an alcoholic haze.

"There is something we must discuss," William replied.

"Come to my office," JH said, not having the vaguest notion as to what was happening.

His factotum came up to the three men as they moved through the outer desks, but William waved him aside.

"We have some bad news, and we must act quickly," William said.

JH just stood there while Gilbert closed the door.

"My son has died, and we need to tell his wife and your family," he continued.

JH sat down, trying to hide a smile on his face.

"How? Where? When? I saw him at dinner last night; he seemed fine then."

"He went back to the office and apparently cut his hand badly on some broken glass and bled to death because no one was there to help him," William said in a neutral tone.

"Cut himself on some broken glass? Never heard that before. You sure?"

"That's what the coroner will say when he issues the death certificate."

Broken glass, my sputonia; we'll see, thought JH.

"We need to get uptown now and let your family know before someone else does," William said, with a little more urgency.

The three men quickly hailed a hansom carriage and sped north.

They were too late; the newspapermen were milling around the front door of the house when they arrived.

"What's the real story?" one reporter shouted. Two more shouted questions at the men as they pushed through the crowd.

Arthur, the butler, opened the door quickly, as if he was expecting them, and they rushed into the mansion.

Mother and new widow were waiting for them in the main hall.

"What happened?" Cynthia, the new widow, asked, turning first to her father, then to William, and finally to Henry.

The oldest man answered her.

"Your husband's dead; he cut his hand on some broken glass and bled to death."

"Broken glass—where and when?"

"In his office, last night."

Cynthia took the news more calmly than her mother, who cried out.

Cynthia was tall and thin, with light brown hair, a sharp nose, and wide eyes. All her life, people remarked how serene and in control she was.

Cynthia had many friends but no intimate companions. She shared some confidences with her brother but kept secrets throughout her life. But even her brother did not know why she chose to marry William Jr. It was a secret shared between husband and wife, and both went to their graves, in separate cemeteries, without revealing it to her family.

Lavinia began to cry, not because of William Jr.'s death, but because it was expected of her. She was a woman who all her life did what was expected of her, obliging one and all by dying when they thought her time was up.

Now, she ushered all of them into the big drawing room, where Arthur had put out liquor and tea.

The men poured drinks for themselves, surprised when Cynthia drew a glass for herself. Her mother said nothing, and she drank it as if used to the taste and resulting rush.

Cynthia did not shed a tear nor show any outward emotions.

Throughout the afternoon and into the evening, William used the telephone to make arrangements, being careful with his words, knowing an operator was listening in.

When J III arrived shortly after five, he ran the gauntlet of reporters, not quite knowing what was happening.

By then, Arthur had sent the houseboy out the back door to buy the evening papers.

"Prescott Son Dead," read one headline.

"Dies Alone," read another.

"Police Investigating," led another paper.

All the stories, however, seem to be accepting the broken glass story.

Henry and William looked at each other, then silently thanked Gilbert and Beatty.

After a quiet supper eaten with little conversation, William and Henry departed by the back entrance.

They made it back to the East Orange house, where Gilbert was waiting.

Funeral arrangements were made, as were plans for the inevitable reception afterwards.

Reverend Adolphus Grambs came by late in the evening, and it was decided to have a quiet service at his Grace Episcopal Church on Main Street within two days.

Where to bury William Jr. was a problem.

Henry had been thinking about his own final resting place, but as yet had made no plans.

Grambs suggested the new Ferndale Cemetery in West Orange.

The next day, father and grandfather went there and bought a twenty-four-grave plot.

Over the years, thirteen Prescott family members would be buried there, and memorials to two others whose bodies were never found were added.

Stoic to the extreme, Henry carried out all of the negotiations, even ordering what would be carved on the tombstone.

Meanwhile, back in New York, Cynthia confused her mother by failing to cry or show any emotion, not even when two seamstresses came to sew appropriate black dresses for both women.

By the day of the funeral, the reporters were gone, and only small items about the funeral appeared in the press.

The world forgot about William Jr. almost overnight, for which everyone was happy.

The following week, Gilbert met with Beatty, handing him $1,500 at Henry's direction.

"On behalf of the family, I thank you," Gilbert said.

"On behalf of my family, I thank you," was the reply.

"Do you have any leads on who killed him?"

"Well, each time he kills, I get a little closer."

Beatty didn't say he had been quietly checking shipping records and was beginning to see a pattern. He had narrowed his search down to the crews of three ships whose arrivals and departures matched the killings.

A year and two deaths later, Beatty caught up with the sailor returning to his ship and quietly sapped him with a woolen sock filled with lead balls. Beatty took the unconscious man to the edge of the East River and rolled him into the waters. He never came up, and Beatty marked the case closed.

Cynthia Basford Prescott 1890

A month after William Jr.'s funeral, Cynthia sat down with her mother and delivered rather startling news.

"I'm pregnant," she said in an even tone.

"Oh, my dear!"

"I've missed my period two months now, and I am pretty sure."

The next day, a doctor confirmed that indeed a baby was on the way.

JH and HJ were delighted. They both hoped for a boy but wondered how they would tell the Prescott men.

Cynthia ended the speculation by journeying alone to East Orange and telling them herself.

Henry and William were shocked and pleased, both hoping it would be a boy.

The Prescott family name would continue if it was a male child.

After the initial congratulations were over, Cynthia spoke up.

"I don't know the contents of my husband's will, but I expect there will be quite a lot of money coming to me."

There was an awkward silence.

Henry spoke up first.

"Actually, he didn't have a will because he had very little property or interest in Prescotts."

William stepped in quickly. "We gave him $25,000 when you married, but quite frankly, we haven't found any of the monies in his accounts."

Cynthia had suspected as much and was prepared.

"I am carrying your grandchild, and I don't want to raise him in my father's house."

This stunned both men.

"Where do you want to raise him?" asked William.

"There is a small house on Barrow Street up for sale. I want to you to buy it and move me there."

Henry and William looked at each other.

"A house on Barrow Street. That's Greenwich Village. You were raised uptown; perhaps a nice house off of Fifth Avenue would be better?"

Cynthia knew she had won. They were arguing location, not the idea.

"I want to go to school, to New York University, and if I lived with my father, he would not permit it."

William took a hard look at his daughter-in-law and decided he had underestimated her.

"What will your father say? I'm sure he is anxious to see his first grandchild brought up as he was," Henry interjected.

"That's one of the reasons I want to move somewhat away from him and my mother."

After much discussion, the two Prescott men agreed but told Cynthia she would have to tell her parents.

The two men did extract one concession. If the child was a boy, she would name him William. For this they were happy, and she did not care.

Cynthia inwardly smiled, thinking about their reaction and enjoying the thought.

William III was born in December 1890.

Cynthia moved into the Barrow Street house in mid-January, just before a major storm blanketed the city.

She had a maid and a nurse, an Irish immigrant recommended by Detective Beatty. Mary Patricia Donovan would remain in service to the Prescott family for more than forty years and through three generations. She would never marry, but through the family, she arranged for the education of four nephews. All four graduated from Fordham University, which received generous support from the Prescott family and her savings.

Beatty and Mary Pat did very well for that university, even though neither had gone beyond grammar school.

Mary Pat was not a particularly religious Irish Catholic and would see many things during her years of service.

Cynthia not only got the house but also received a generous allowance from both sets of grandparents.

She took up painting, attended classes at NYU, and quickly became part of the floating bohemian crowd that coalesced in the Greenwich Village as the century waned.

Cynthia did not nurse William III and left much of the caretaking to Mary Pat. While the nurses often changed, Mary Pat was the constant in William III's life.

His mother soon found the companion she had sought all her life.

Greenwich Village was at that time a mixture of professors and professional men, their families, and artists and writers. There were Italians on many blocks hard by rich families who surrounded Washington Square with their Federal Era homes.

Henry James would make one such house famous in his novel *Washington Square*. Other houses were owned by families through generations. Many of those families went each Sunday up Broadway to the new Grace Episcopal Church.

It was here, during a Sunday service, that Cynthia met Edna Boardman, called Sydney by her more intimate friends.

The two were in bed in Sydney's townhouse, the family and servants blessedly gone to Long Branch for the August hot period.

"Why did you marry your husband?" Sydney asked.

"Because I knew what he was, and I knew what I was," she said looking down at Sydney's round breasts.

"How did you know?"

Cynthia laughed. "Like I knew what you are."

She rolled over and lay on her back, thinking of her honeymoon night.

They were in Saratoga, at the Parque Hotel.

The wedding was a day earlier, and they had arrived at the honeymoon suite after the journey from the city.

"We should go to bed," William Jr. said.

Cynthia was at the dresser desk, combing her hair.

"Yes, we should, but I think we should talk first."

"About what?"

"About us, and who we are."

"We're two people in love."

"No, Willie, we like each other, but we don't love each other."

William was perplexed but also a little frightened.

"What do you mean?"

"Oh, Willie, do you not realize I know you like boys better than girls?"

William Jr. was startled and a loss for words.

"Then why did you marry me?"

"Because I like girls better than boys."

William Jr. was even more shaken.

"Now, don't worry; I am prepared to let you have your thing, but don't expect me not to have my fun."

A visibly frightened William Jr. continued to remain silent. This supposedly cloistered girl, no woman, was revealing to him that she knew his deepest secret.

"Now, we are man and wife, and what goes on here in our bedroom will remain our secret. I don't like men touching me, and you like boys. But my parents and your father and grandfather expect to have heirs. So we must come to an arrangement."

Again, a speechless William Jr. looked at his bride with new respect and a little fear.

"So what do we do?" he said in a quiet voice.

"Well, for one thing, we must show some blood on the sheets tonight, or the staff will talk."

"And then?"

"Until we have made a child we will do the things other couples do once a month, when I think it is the best time to create him or her. After that, we will remain a couple in name only."

William Jr. stammered some words and went into the bathroom, realizing his greatest fear had been alleviated, and his fondest hopes had been realized.

Sydney turned to Cynthia and asked, "Did you murder your husband?"

"No, but it worked out very well for both of us," she said reaching for the buxom woman again.

Thomas Beatty 1891

As the sailor's body slipped into the East River of Manhattan, Thomas Beatty gave a grunt of relief.

It had taken him another year since the Prescott murder to track down this elusive killer of posh men, and he reveled in the justice he had delivered.

Beatty was a man of rigid morals and viewed life as a matter of right and wrong.

Things were either right or wrong. There was no gray for him.

One of his sisters told him in anger one day that he should be a priest.

He smiled at her and said nothing.

Only his distaste for priests prevented him from becoming one himself.

Three sessions butt upright with Father Mulroney had cured the thirteen-year-old Beatty of respect for the mother church.

It did not change his rigorous channeling of all actions into good or bad, nor his conviction of where he would eventually be consigned—heaven or hell. While Beatty never went to confession or church, his mother and sisters prayed daily for a miracle.

Beatty knew that when his time came the Lord would tote up his deeds and make a final judgment. Convinced he was on the side of the angels, he didn't worry about that day.

He had spent the first fourteen years at St. Michael's School in the West Village and the next eight years making money in any nefarious way he could.

Since he mostly stole from people he perceived as greedy or crooked, his mind was at ease.

Those eight years gave him an extensive knowledge as to how the criminal element worked on the island.

It also gave him a healthy dislike of most rich people, whom he saw as exploiters of the Irish, Italian, and other immigrant groups then flooding New York.

Rather, he joined the New York City Police Department as almost its first Irish recruit, at the age of twenty-two.

But that did not prevent him from learning how to use his position to aid his relatives and himself, as well as the Irish population at large.

Early in his career, while walking a beat just off Broadway on Thirteenth Street, he had come upon a well-dressed man attempting to kiss a woman. She was fending him off, and Beatty quickly knocked him senseless with his gosh.

Hauling the man to the old muster house on Fourteenth Street, he shackled him to a chair.

His captain came over, saw the man, and just as quickly released him.

"He's not for here," he said.

"Why not?"

"'Cause he's a Malcolm, and we don't arrest people like the Malcolms."

"Why not?"

"Do you like your job and beat and want to stay here long enough to get a proper uniform?"

"So what will happen now?"

"Someone from downtown will call on him tomorrow at home, and next week there'll be some extra money in your pay and mine."

That was exactly what happened, and Beatty also got a visitor.

John Murray was the fixer for the Democratic Party when a matter concerned the police.

Tall, fat, and well dressed, he approached Beatty as he left his headquarters one night.

"You kept your mouth closed last week."

"Didn't seem like a good idea to say anything."

"Right, right. So let's talk."

"About what?"

"About you."

"I'm a patrol officer."

"I've checked you out, and people say you're smart and incorruptible."

"I just see what's right and what's wrong."

"Sure, sure, I know that, but there's more to living in this city than that. And y
ou're one of the few smart Irish dingoes around here right now."

"I get paid no more than the others here, and I don't take bribes like the others."

"We at Tammany know that, but sooner or later you'll have to make some compromises."

"When I do, I'll quit."

"No need for that. The Wigwam works with everyone, especially if they're Irish."

"Not me."

"Look, you'll either work with us or be gone, and that can happen tomorrow if we don't reach an understanding tonight."

"What kind of understanding?"

"Some of the fellas think we need some smart policemen who can work the system and help us bring in more Irishmen onto the rolls."

"We need more Micks."

"And we need more smart ones up the ladder."

"And you think I'm one of them."

"Oh, I wouldn't be here if we didn't."

"That's so."

"Here's my offer. The Wigwam has certain strings in the police, and we want to use them for you."

"The Wigwam" was the everyday name for the Democratic Party house in Lower Manhattan called Tammany Hall.

"And in return?"

"You help us."

"I don't do anything crooked."

"No need. We just want to make sure our people get hired and promoted, and when certain jobs are needed, they get done."

"I don't do crooked," he said with more force.

"We'll never ask you to do that. We have others to do those jobs. We want to use your sense of justice to get justice. Sometimes we all have to do more than let the judges and juries decide."

Having already seen how easy it was to buy a verdict, Beatty began to listen more closely.

"Too many of our people are dying or going to jail because some of those rich people are flouting the law."

"I know that, and I don't see how I can help."

"Agree to work with us, and we'll show you. Think about it, and we'll meet again tomorrow."

Beatty thought about the conversation all night and into the morning.

He had no one to trust on the force, so he went to Michael O'Connor, the unofficial mayor of the Irish in the West Village.

No one knew how old O'Connor was, and he didn't know for sure. Landing in New York in the 1840s, he was a roustabout, stevedore, shop owner, and finally financier of numerous Irish bars and brothels. By this time, he held court in an Irish bar near the docks on Dean Street.

"You've been talked to by the Wigwam," O'Connor started the conversation.

"I thought you might know."

"I recommended you to them. You're a smart lad with a smart head."

"You know how I feel about things."

"So do they. But you have something we all need—a sense of justice."

"It could get me into trouble."

"That's what the Wigwam is there for, to get you out of trouble."

"Just like you did."

"I suppose so."

Beatty was referring to the time when Beatty was seventeen and heard his eleven-year-old cousin Maureen had been raped by her uncle.

Without saying a word, he went to the uncle's house and started to beat him with his fists. Beatty beat him so hard the man died at his feet.

Not knowing what to do, he ran to O'Connor. The older man arranged everything, and the authorities ruled the death a heart attack.

Maureen, traumatized by the attack, was never the same again and finally committed suicide seven years later.

No one ever spoke of the incident, but Beatty noticed how people moved respectfully away from him.

It was O'Connor who arranged for him to join the police.

"You're a rare individual even for an Irishmen, and right now we have need of someone like you."

Murray met with Beatty, and they agreed he would work for Tammany Hall, or as the natives said, the Wigwam.

From that moment on, Beatty's rise in the force, beginning to be known as "the "Department," began.

Within two years he was a sergeant and three years later a lieutenant.

Those five years were spent working on incidents involving rich patrons and friends of the Wigwam.

Early on, he began keeping notebooks on what he did, who was involved, and what the outcome was.

Murray arranged for him to be dressed in good clothes and to learn how to talk in a manner that more educated and richer people spoke in.

By 1885, Beatty was the person the Wigwam used on its more sensitive cases.

During that time, Beatty also quietly disposed of four men whose crimes were obvious, but where convictions were not possible.

Three of them involved crooked lawyers who added murder to their more venal crimes.

The fourth was the son of a Fifth Avenue millionaire who twice bought his innocence for raping Irish maids.

Beatty lured him to a supposed tryst with one of his victims and strangled him in the bedroom. He left him hanging there, and no matter what the father did to find out who murdered his son, Beatty escaped punishment.

What he did for the Wigwam burnished his reputation as an honest copper, but also one who could be judge and executioner. He was also the recipient of much information of use to the leaders in fending off any attempts at reforms.

In 1886, Beatty was assigned to the newly formed murder section and quickly gained a reputation for solving fatal crimes.

More importantly, in a city with twenty-eight newspapers fighting for juicy news, he knew how to keep people out of the headlines.

In several instances, he solved crimes without publicizing the sordid details as to why the victim, usually a man, was in that particular place.

The archbishop (later cardinal) was particularly happy he managed to convict a prostitute for the murder of a priest with whom she was performing her services.

In this instance, her pimp accidently killed him while trying to rob the poor man.

By offering a deal and getting them to plead before a friendly judge, the papers never found out.

The priest was buried as the victim of a heart attack.

Beatty ignored the invitation from the archbishop to meet until O'Connor told him to go.

It was the last time he talked to the old man. O'Connor died in 1887 and was buried in Woodlawn Cemetery. The next day, Beatty bought the adjoining plots and eventually joined him.

By the time of William Jr.'s murder in 1890, Beatty was an important part of the New York Police. He was a captain and was known as man not to be trifled with, either physically or politically.

Theodore Roosevelt became police commissioner in May 1895.

One of his first acts was to send for Beatty.

"You're a wretch for Tammany Hall," he said in his usual bullying manner.

"Perhaps," was all Beatty could say.

"Well, you have a choice; work with me to make this police force something to be proud of, or resign.

"You can't make me."

"Oh yes I can, but it's not what I want. I know you have notebooks on everything, and I also know you're incorruptible. So come work for me and not tell those yeggs downtown anything, or get out."

Batty thought for a minute, the two men glaring at each other.

"What's in this for me? You'll leave, and I'll be left with the legacy of being a traitor."

"When I leave, you come with me."

Thus was born a partnership that took Beatty to Cuba, the White House, and eventually to a sinecure with the Prescotts and other important families.

Roosevelt cleaned up the police force and laid the groundwork for the anticorruption task force two years later.

With Beatty at his side, TR went on midnight tours of the city with the muckraking newspaperman Jacob Riis to check up on his officers and catch lazy cops. And he did catch lazy cops—lots of them.

But in the process, he was forced to explore the entire Lower East Side of Manhattan, with its overcrowded tenements, its unsanitary conditions, and its oppressive labor practices. TR met exploited immigrants and toured unsafe factories. He witnessed firsthand the consequences of inadequate health care and pension coverage.

Some biographers argue that this was the beginning of change in TR's political outlook and the start of his progressive agenda.

To Beatty, these conditions were all too familiar, but he saw them with new eyes as he strolled through the city with Roosevelt.

True to his word, Roosevelt took Beatty with him as bodyguard and confidant.

Beatty was a guest at Sagamore, Roosevelt's home, and became friendly with his wife, Edith, and his children.

Theodore Roosevelt Jr. became a lifelong friend and was at Beatty's funeral.

Beatty's grandnephew Thomas was with the young Roosevelt when he suffered a fatal heart attack in Normandy a month after the June 6 D-Day invasion.

When Roosevelt left the White House and went on his famous trips to Africa and South America, Beatty opened an office in New York. By that time, his notebooks contained much information useful to people like the Prescotts.

He was retained by them and others to help gather information and to keep unfavorable news about family members from the press.

Having never married, Beatty used his connections to help his nieces and nephews.

Kevin, the oldest, eventually headed the Chicago office of Prescotts.

Rod became the chief accountant of the theater chain.

Sean became private secretary to James Jr. and eventually secretary of the corporation.

Beatty's niece Maureen married a man who also became a captain in the police force but was convicted of bribery during an 1897 corruption scandal. He went to prison and was stabbed to death within a year.

Beatty supported Maureen and her children until they grew up.

These grandnephews, the three Hennessey brothers, went to Fordham University and also joined Prescotts. They rose in the organization to very high levels and displayed a loyalty to the founding family through both the good and the bad times.

Eileen, the youngest grandniece and his favorite, became a nurse and went to France in 1917 with the troops, married a Frenchmen she met there, and lived the rest of her life in Paris.

He missed her most of all.

In 1922, while walking on Dean Street near where O'Connor's old bar stood, Beatty suffered a heart attack and died on the sidewalk.

There were many people at his funeral, and no one noticed the grave next to his.

It was Mary Pat Donovan's.

Rebecca Prescott 1892

William Sr., often called "the Colonel," came to a decision one night alone in his bedroom.

In 1892, the continuance of the Prescott name and family rested with Becky. She seemed not interested in any of the suitors beating a path to her East Orange home.

Having learned about his daughter-in-law's sexual dalliances thanks to Beatty, he was concerned about his daughter and the future of Prescotts.

Sent to private schools and then Wellesley College, she seemed to be drifting.

William Sr. did not know of her longtime affair with Abraham.

In her mind, the future belonged with him. How to make this happen was still unclear.

Of James, she thought little. Seeing him around the house office made him both familiar and yet a stranger.

By the time she was twenty, Abraham Gilbert had poked her in all three openings and she had enjoyed it, starting with their first time in her bedroom one Saturday when the house was deserted.

That time had happened almost by accident, when her mother's usual gathering was postponed for a christening of some acquaintance.

With the staff off, Abraham and she had been left alone almost through inattention.

Having had intense feelings almost since puberty, they consummated their first act almost in awe of each other.

It was enough to give them a lifelong attachment.

Both knew there were many barriers to marriage, but with the optimism of youth, they did not worry about the future.

When Becky was twenty-three and still unmarried, her father stepped in.

She was stunned when her father sat down with her one Saturday and asked if she was considering marrying James.

On her part, there had never been a thought.

"You've not liked any of the men who have come around."

"They're so immature and not very smart," she replied.

"Perhaps you need an older man?"

"What older men do I know?"

"James."

"Are you really thinking of him?"

"Yes, I am, for three reasons. He's smart. He's attractive. He would make a good husband."

Becky's mind was racing

"What does James think?"

"I haven't asked him yet."

"Perhaps you should."

"I will, if you are acceptable to the idea."

"Well, let's say I'm not opposed to the idea. He is rather attractive."

"Then I'll discuss it with him."

"You do that, but remind him that he needs to court me and not assume I will fall into his arms."

"I think he will like the idea."

William's approach to James occurred two months after Angela left for Sicily.

Heartbroken and still a little shaken from the beating he had received, James was open to the proposal.

For the next five months, he courted the far-from-reluctant Becky. Their engagement was announced around Thanksgiving time.

During their courtship, Becky and James learned to be circumspect with each other.

He did not tell her about Angela, and she hinted at liaisons but gave no specifics.

"I'm not a virgin," she said to him one night.

"I respect that; neither am I."

"I'm sure of that."

"We will learn to love each other."

"Perhaps, but I expect to be respected and cherished. You're marrying me for a chance to have the Prescott money."

"I don't think your father has that in mind."

"I think he will protect our children."

"I can live with that."

"You'll have to, but he's determined we marry."

"Only if you agree."

"I think it will work, but don't ask me about the past."

"No need. The past is the past."

After sending Beatty to Belfast and learning about James's past, William Sr. had misgivings but decided he was still the best choice for his daughter.

He also made it clear he was entailing Prescotts for his grandchildren.

"You'll have a generous allowance, but you will never own one part of Prescotts."

James had expected this condition. The other condition surprised him.

William Sr. made one other request of James.

"You haven't gotten your citizenship papers yet, and I want you to. And when you do, I want you to take the name James Camaron Prescott."

James thought for a moment, then said quietly that he would.

The couple married in the Grace Episcopal Church of East Orange.

Two nights before, Becky and Abraham spent most of the night together in New York at a hotel while she was on a shopping trip.

She promised the marriage would not make a difference in their relationship.

In fact, the marriage provided the perfect cover for their dalliances, which lasted until his death.

James on his side eventually lived a double life—in East Orange with Becky and in New York City with Angela.

Becky's dalliances with Abraham led to one complication she had not expected.

When she became pregnant and t

hroughout her pregnancy, she worried that the child might be Abraham's.

She had slept with James and Abraham on successive days and discovered she was pregnant a month later.

The fear almost ruined her maternity period, so the tears flowed freely as the baby was swathed in blankets. The boy had pale skin and resembled James.

Everyone thought they were tears of joy, and she did not dissuade them.

Henry Prescott Sr. 1892

During a private meeting at the beginning of the year, Henry and William laid out their plans for Prescott, and what they expected his two acolytes to do.

"We are gradually going to get out of the merchant business," Henry said in a sad voice, because it was the basis of the family fortune.

"There are too many new department stores and distributors moving in. Soon, we would either need to expand or go broke. Our banks are doing well, and they will continue to do well as long as we keep them local and conservative. We'll lend only to those people we know and not have too much tied up in one person or group. What we will do is start investing more in new inventions and ideas."

The other two men nodded in agreement. They couldn't fault the Colonel's ability to sniff out potential new inventions. He had a few failures, but his support of Morgenthaler, Ives, and others had proven very profitable.

They also recognized Henry was extremely frail, spending more time in bed than at his desk.

They were seated in his original office. Henry was too frail to leave the house.

Henry had kept to the East Orange house, welcoming a steady line of men who showed him what they had conceived. He had a pipeline stretching all the way to Chicago and beyond. Having banks in cities remote from metropolises helped.

"We will stick with what we know: distribution, shipping, banking, and printing. I have been talking to a man named Richard Warren Sears who is thinking of taking on Montgomery Ward in the catalog business. I think his ideas will work. James, your next assignment is to go to Chicago and help him get it off the ground," said William.

James nodded, unhappy to be leaving Becky while she was pregnant, and even unhappier to be leaving Angela.

With his usual thoroughness, and thanks to Beatty, the Colonel knew about the woman in New York. He was satisfied Becky was happy but wondered why that was so. Surely his daughter knew something, but she appeared unconcerned.

Henry was kept in the dark.

He also trusted Beatty to find out what happened to Mary Blume. Calling herself the widowed Mrs. Cassiday, she owned a hotel and bar in Utica, New York. His son was growing into a tall, robust man and stood to inherit a thriving enterprise.

"She used that $5,000 well," he smiled to himself when informed by Beatty.

Unaware of his wife's knowledge, he felt he had done right by his family and Mary Blume. He had no desire to see or know more about his son. As far as he was concerned, that incident was closed.

With his wife gone, his life focused on the company.

The Colonel was consumed with growing Prescotts. He also recognized his father was dying. So did the older man.

Over the past months, the elderly man had signed over all properties and stocks to the Colonel.

While they still talked often, Henry had withdrawn from the business, sitting in his rooms reflecting on a life spent creating the building blocks of a great enterprise.

His only son was carrying on the business, and he knew it was in good hands.

Henry looked at Gilbert and congratulated himself in the choice of helpmate for his son.

He viewed James as an adventurer who had found treasure but was chained to it for the rest of his life.

There was at least one grandson to carry on the name, and his second grandchild was on its way. He hoped to see if it was a boy or a girl.

Prescotts was changing, and in a way he hoped he would not live to see those changes.

"My father was a merchant and I was a merchant, but the future is in other areas," he mused to himself.

Shipping was an addition to Prescotts, brought about by a new relationship that the Colonel had developed.

Through Grambs at Grace Episcopal Church, the Colonel was introduced to a rising financier named John P. Morgan. Morgan awakened his interest in shipping. Always cautious, he invested with Morgan on a number of deals, appreciating the man's ability to rationalize companies to form extremely competitive business enterprises.

In these ventures, William Sr. did not risk more than he could afford to lose. To date, almost all had turned out well. He was still wary of the crowd around Morgan and knew they would turn on him in a minute.

One area of particular interest to him was shipping. He had avoided the financial machinations associated with railroad building and financing. But shipping was a different thing.

His success in the printing industry made him focus there, but he was building his knowledge in this new area.

In the meantime, there was the need to send James to study what Sears was planning to do.

James left the meeting thinking how he might turn his trips to Chicago into more time with Angela.

Becky did not seem overly concerned with James's new assignment, almost seeming to welcome it.

Angela was a little unhappy and worried.

"When will I see you?"

"Before and after every trip."

"How?"

"I will say I am leaving a day earlier and come back a day later. We'll have two days together."

"But you'll be gone for weeks."

"It's not to be helped. It's what I do and will be doing for the next few years."

"I'll miss you, and so will Joseph."

"He's not old enough to miss me."

"He will."

True to his word, James left the house in East Orange a day ahead and the three spent a warm spring day in the city.

She saw him off on the train with Joseph in tow. The boy cried as the train pulled out.

For almost a year, James kept up the commute, and it was probably the most time he spent with his mistress and child for years.

Henry Prescott 1893

The doctors tried to sound encouraging, but Henry knew his time was near. In his lifetime, America had changed, but he had remained steadfast in his vision and principles. Prescotts was a far different enterprise than when he took over from his father.

He thought of the man, of his secrets, and wondered if anyone had divined the man. He certainly hadn't. Of his mother, there was the faded tintype of her on his dresser and some memories, but little else. He thought she instilled a sense of honesty, but his acumen clearly came from his father.

He thought of Rebecca and their walks in Knowland's Knoll. He remembered her eyes, and the way she dipped her head when speaking with others. He thought of their fierce lovemaking, and the joy she gave him in this bedroom.

We spend our lives and get back bits and pieces of other people, he mused.

"She gave me everything," he said aloud, startling the woman at his bedside. He looked at her, remembering she was his grandson's keeper, but knowing she was becoming more than that to the Prescotts.

I guess I will lie next to my son and Rebecca soon, he thought.

The woman, Mary Patricia Donovan, got up and fussed with his pillows.

"Lie quietly, Mr. Prescott; conserve your strength," she said.

"Conserve it for what?" he replied gruffly.

"To get better."

"You know I won't, and I know that as well."

"Your son will be here tonight, and your granddaughter is in her room."

"Have her come in, and then leave us alone."

The woman did as she was told, and Rebecca joined him.

"I know you have your secrets, and I don't want to know them. But you need to protect the Prescott name and help build a dynasty," he told her as she sat by the bed.

Becky did not reply but sat silently, heavy with child and fearful of what the old man was saying.

"Your father is no fool, and neither is that child watcher out in the hall. What you do will affect all of us, so be careful."

Rebecca held back tears, fearful of what he would say next.

"You be careful, that's all I am going to say."

The Colonel came that night and sat by the bed.

"Do you know when I knew you would be a great leader?" Henry said.

The Colonel did not reply.

"When you went up to Connecticut and fired those men. I knew then you would do well for me and for Prescotts."

"You never said a word."

"Didn't need to. You did it. Even went without breakfast that day."

"Gilbert helped."

"I knew he would be a great helpmate. You do right by him."

"I have and I will."

"Prescotts is yours now. I made up for whatever sins your grandfather committed and kept us honest. I want you to do the same."

"I will."

"I know you will. Now leave me in peace. I'm tired."

It was the last conversation between father and son. Henry died that night, dreaming of Rebecca and strolling on Knowland's Knoll.

The funeral was well attended, with many of the surviving men whom he had done business with in attendance.

They spoke of his ability to drive a hard bargain but also of his commitment to keeping it once struck.

As he wished, he was buried beside Rebecca in Ferndale Cemetery. His daughter-in-law did not attend, but her mother and brother were there, as was the Gilbert family.

The Newark Eagle ran a long obituary about him but ruined the tribute by mentioning his father's early efforts at running the embargo during the War of 1812.

A lifetime of good works could not erase his heritage.

JH Basford 1895

JH was not happy as he tore the January 1895 page from the Currier & Ives calendar on his wall. It was a special edition presented to him as a board member of the Wheeling & Susquehanna Railroad. It depicted a W&S coal train moving through the Berkshire Cut in lower Pennsylvania. The picture captured the only reason for the railroad's existence: Coal from the region had just one route through the Allegheny Mountains, and it was controlled by his railroad. JH considered it his railroad because he had sunk much of his family's wealth into secretly buying most of its stock.

Within a few weeks, he expected to show his shares at the annual meeting and take the chairman's seat.

None of his fellow directors knew of his actions or plans.

After demonstrating his power, JH was determined to throw them off the board and put in people beholden to him. Choosing whom to ask required both tact and discretion. But few people in New York really believed in anything JH did.

So the list he held in his hand had few names. At a family gathering during Christmas, he had approached William Prescott to sit on the board but was turned down flat.

"We stick to what we know best," was the Colonel's reason behind the decision.

JH hated the Prescotts—hated their way of making money and hated the fact that his grandson had some Jewish blood in him.

Yes, JH knew of Sarah's background and even begrudged her her training as a doctor.

He snickered at the way they covered up her death. But even after her death she had worked against him. A female doctor, Helen Utterman, whom Sarah trained attended Cynthia in the birth of his first grandson. The Prescotts had insisted on her because of Sarah's confidence.

Lavinia and Cynthia had both insisted on her, primarily because Dr. Utterman was being recognized more and more as one of America's most knowledgeable doctors on childbirth. Most of her ideas originated with Sarah, but she was better able to push them.

More and more it was being recognized that hospitals were a breeding ground for illnesses for both mothers and newborn infants.

With the help of William Prescott's funding, the clinic in East Orange was becoming a model for better maternity care.

JH hated the fact Cynthia gave birth in the clinic and was immediately driven home to the Prescott house to recover.

All the women he knew went to the Parker Pavilion and stayed there for a week, receiving visitors, cards, flowers, and whatnots.

Not so his daughter, who, even after returning to her New York home, remained strangely distant and appeared only infrequently at the house or at family events.

On Dr. Utterman's orders, Cynthia went home the next day.

Returning to New York a month later, she hired a nurse and sort-of nanny and went about her business. What those activities were, JH had no idea, and his wife just shrugged when he thought to ask.

Cynthia appeared to reject JH's notion of how to do things. She gave no parties; she did not attend Sunday dinners or even try to entertain in the manner JH would have liked.

Even William III's first birthdays were muted affairs held in the gloomy—to JH—house on Barrow Street.

Another thing bothering JH about his grandson was the woman who was his primary caregiver, Mary Pat.

"She's probably filling him with that Papist pap," he thought.

Turning away from his grandson, JH went to his desk and once more examined the list of men he thought could serve on a board where he would command.

JH's interest in the W&S coincided with the death of his father two years prior.

With the death came a new freedom for JH.

He came back from the funeral and fired the three men who had been both caretakers and spies for his father.

He didn't replace them but rather started managing the business himself.

As a result of his newfound attention to business, his lunch and afternoon sojourns to the Union League Club had been curtailed.

Feeling surprisingly energetic for the first time in years, he threw himself into work.

Lavinia noticed the difference and was secretly pleased. Cynthia didn't care, and J III remained happily oblivious.

JH had kept his efforts secret by teaming with the National Bank of Illinois in Chicago and its vice president, Jacob Guttman.

JH had convinced Guttman to advance him monies for his stock purchases and even colluded in buying them under the names of bank depositors. These individuals, mostly wealthy Chicagoans of German descent, did not know they were the straw men for JH.

The plan was to transfer all of the stocks to JH a day before the annual meeting on March 15.

When drawing up their scheme, Guttman mentioned the fact that the target date was also the ides of March.

Brushing aside the allusion, JH spent a comfortable night in Chicago, enjoying the company of a woman Guttman had procured.

When JH tore the February page from the calendar, he was even more pleased, as it seemed his scheme was still secret.

A telegram from Chicago upset him that afternoon. It was from Guttman, who asked him to deposit $250,000 in the bank "to cover our expenses."

Perplexed, he wired back for an explanation. The return telegram said a letter was coming by special messenger.

For two days, JH quietly fumed.

The letter was short but specific.

"Need funds to cover shortage in accounts with stocks we are holding," was all it basically said.

JH spent the next two days pulling together the funds, liquidating many of the family's holdings to do so.

When they were dispatched, JH sat back and wondered.

He almost strangled when another telegram arrived demand the same amount again.

Again the telegram hinted at the need to protect their investment.

When March 14 came, JH ordered the stocks transferred as agreed.

Guttman was strangely silent.

That night he sent a frantic telegram to Guttman that was unanswered.

JH spent a sleepless night and went to the board meeting without the stocks in hand.

By then he had calculated he owned just 38 percent of the outstanding stock, and those Chicago burghers held the other 14 percent.

He sat quietly through the meeting and said almost nothing. When it was adjourned, he went directly to the new Grand Central Station and boarded a train to Chicago.

Guttman met him at the station, and the two went quickly to the bank.

In his office, Guttman explained the stocks were still in the accounts because he couldn't transfer them.

"We have had some trouble making the accounts balance, and the Clearing House of Chicago was asking too many questions."

"You mean they have the stocks that I paid for?"

Guttman nodded and shrugged.

JH went home on the next train.

Within weeks, rumors of the First National Bank's troubles began to circulate.

JH could do nothing, and when the failed, he lost the stocks and the money he had sent Guttman.

That December, the bank failed, soon followed by forty other Illinois banks. Guttman had lent money to men building the Calumet Electric Street Railway and some construction suppliers.

He committed suicide soon after.

By the time JH torn the January page from his new calendar with the same picture, he faced ruin.

He had paid $5 a share for his W&S stock, and it was trading at less than a dollar.

What's more, the Pennsylvania Railroad had come to the board and told board members—not asked—to sell the company for fifty cents a share.

The "Pennsy" had a huge hammer over the company. Its president said to the assembled board members that, if they did not sell to him, he intended to drive a tunnel through the mountains and put them out of business.

Within twenty-four hours, the deal was done, and JH stared gloomily at the future.

He knew the other directors would smell a rat when they finally tallied ownership shares and discovered that he owned 38 percent of the company.

JH went to the Union League Club and drank for an hour.

He finished his last drink and walked out on Fourteenth Street directly onto the traction tracks in front of a trolley. He was killed instantly.

William was not surprised when he heard the news.

Ever since JH asked him to join the W&S board, he had made it his business to keep abreast of the W&S. As the stock declined, he had calculated how much JH was losing.

As JH liquidated, he bought. In fact, if he figured right, almost all of the family's holdings were now held by Prescotts.

He rushed to the Basford house, running through the gathered group of reporters, remembering the day his son died.

Lavinia was crying quietly, her son by her side.

She looked at him with red eyes and cried harder.

J III seemed shaken but in better control than his mother.

"What do we do?" he asked.

"First, we keep to the idea it was an accident," William replied.

"How do we manage the business?"

"I'll send James there tomorrow to sort things out. In the meantime, we prepare for the funeral and keep up a brave front."

J III patted his mother's back. She cried louder. William motioned to Arthur to bring something to drink. The coffee, tea, and liquor appeared almost immediately, as if it was already prepared and waiting.

William wondered where Cynthia was.

The daughter was in bed with her lover when her father died.

She did not come home until past six, to be met at the door by William III and Mary Pat.

The Irish woman stopped Cynthia at the door, holding William III back.

She mouthed the words, "Something has happened."

Cynthia understood and picked up her son.

"Mommy needs to go out again, Billie. Let Mary Pat get you dinner. But first go into the kitchen and find out what cook has for you."

"Your father's had an accident; they want you uptown as soon as you're in," Mary Pat said in a brogue made deeper by her feelings.

"Is it bad?"

"Worse than that!"

"Oh," said Cynthia, turning around and making for the livery stand on Sixth Avenue.

She arrived a little after seven and found the family having a quiet, cold dinner.

"What happened?" she asked.

The facts were quickly told as she sat at the table.

Ironically, William sat in the seat reserved for his son, careful to avoid taking JH's place.

A clergyman arrived after dinner, and funeral arrangements were quickly made. JH was buried two days later, next to his parents.

William took care of everything and rode with the Basfords in their carriage. William III stayed home. Since his relationship with his grandfather was sporadic, he did not feel a sense of loss.

Neither did Cynthia, who wondered only about how the estate was divided and when she could get back to her normal routine—which really meant her lover.

Not expecting to die, JH had made a will leaving everything to J III upon his birth. It was an old will, and the lawyer named as executor had since died.

William seized on this and Beatty's good connections in probate court to get named executor.

After James, Gilbert, and their accountant examined JH's books, they realized there was little money left for the family—certainly not enough to keep them in the style they were accustomed to.

Henry and James made a decision to lie to them.

They told J III there was about $100,000 coming to him, and that Cynthia had an allowance of $5,000 until she was thirty, when $50,000 was due her.

J III was also the beneficiary of Henry's largesse as he arranged for the young man to join a newly formed stock brokerage firm. His way was smoothed by Henry's assurance that the firm would get Prescott business.

He remained with the firm for the rest of his life, dying of cancer at fifty-one without ever marrying.

Henry quietly told Lavinia that her expenses would be met for the rest of her life by him—a promise that he and his son-in-law kept until she died in 1906.

Having watched Cynthia and having used Beatty to check on her activities since his grandchild was born, Henry made her a startling proposal.

"If you allow me to take William III to live with us in East Orange, I will double the yearly allowance," he said a week after the funeral.

Secretly glad to rid herself of motherhood, she withheld her response for more than a minute as if pondering the proposal.

"You'll need to take Mary Pat and the cook with him," she said.

"I know that," Henry said with one eye looking at James. Thanks to Beatty, both men knew a lot more than Cynthia ever suspected about her dalliances and what went on inside the Barrow Street residence.

"I really am torn, but maybe it is for the best."

"I think it is."

"I'll visit him often."

"I'm sure you will."

"How do I explain this to Mother?"

"I'll take care of that."

"I guess it is for the best."

"I'm sure it is."

One week later, Mary Pat, the cook, and William III moved to the house in East Orange, and William now had the grandchild he wanted to mold into the new leader of the family.

For her part, Cynthia threw herself into the Greenwich Village life, becoming a renowned hostess and friend of many writers and artists who passed through over the next thirty years.

At first she visited William III every month. Then it was every three months, and by the time a year had past, she came only for his birthdays.

She missed his graduation from the Hun School.

When he finished at Yale, she made the ceremonies, and then abandoned him to life.

She died in 1921 when the cabin she and her lover occupied in an Elmsford, New York, artist colony caught fire. A lighted cigarette was blamed. Cynthia perished with her lover at the time. Both women were drunk.

William and her brother represented the family at Cynthia's funeral. It was a big event, because many artists and writers she had befriended over the years were there. Willa Cather gave a eulogy, as did other Greenwich Village denizens.

William III said nothing.

Within five years, both Lavinia and J III were dead as well. The Basford family was reduced to William III, and he thought of himself as a Prescott.

Samuel Gilbert 1902

With a continuing hacking cough draining him, Gilbert recognized it was time to retire, and so, at the end of 1902, he stepped down from Prescotts, leaving James in full charge.

"I am the last of the founding generation, and I wish you all well," was how he ended his retirement speech.

The Colonel, frail himself, embraced his and whispered into his ear, "I still remember my promise to you."

"I know," Gilbert whispered back.

After the retirement party, he decided it was time to tell his children and grandchild about the family fortune. He was out of the Prescott empire. For it was indeed now an empire, stretching almost across the country.

Delilah had lived to see their first and probably only grandchild as well as the new century, but she was gone, buried in Ferndale, where he intended to lie beside her. He was feeling old and a little out of touch. The world was moving fast, and he was afraid he was getting left behind.

He had served the Prescott family for more than fifty years. His son Abraham was established, but with little sign of marrying or coming into the business.

Gilbert also knew there was a secret in his son's heart, but he did not know what it was.

Of his other son, there was a fear he would spend his inheritance quickly.

"A father knows his son," Gilbert thought.

Up until now, he had refused to show his financial position to Abraham or anyone else.

He sat in his favorite chair, alone in the house he had shared with his family. His two daughters were gone, as was Bethel, his third son.

"Yes, now is the time. I'll talk to them this week."

The meeting went totally unexpectedly for the patriarch, as Abraham seemed to have known all along of his great wealth.

"What difference does it make?" Abraham was the first to speak.

"You mean I don't have to work?" was Big Billie's comment. Gilbert still could not think of him as a "William."

"Think what this means for Jasmine," was Sabrina's comment.

"I intend to split my inheritance in half. You both get equal shares."

"That's fine with us, but what about the Prescott stock?" asked Abraham.

"That goes half to each, but I hope you will continue to support the family."

"If you had been white, you would have gotten 20 percent," was Abraham's rejoinder.

"If I had been white, I wouldn't have been involved."

"Still, that's little return for all you've done for them."

"I ain't that uppity. It's kept you all comfortable all these years."

"I hope you're with us a long time, Papa Gilbert," said Sabrina, a title she rarely used except around Jasmine.

"I expect so, but it doesn't mean you can't have some money now for whatever you want."

"It will help with Jasmine's lessons and teachers."

"She has the talent in the family."

"Fat good it will do her," Abraham said bitterly.

Gilbert took Sabrina aside and told her to keep her husband working.

"He'll get into trouble if you don't."

"I know that," was all she said.

When Gilbert gave them the first $50,000 that Christmas, Billie quit work the next day and did not take another job the rest of his life.

Within a year, he was out frequently at night, staying away until morning on many occasions.

The next year, Gilbert gave the money to Sabrina to dole out.

Abraham invested his savings and spent little money on himself but helped others.

His affair with Rebecca Prescott consumed his private life, while his business was prosperous and growing.

In an ironic twist, he hired two white accountants along with two Negro graduates.

He was nominated to run for city council by Democrats in Orange, but he failed to get strong support from the party and lost decisively,

During the First World War he was deemed too old to serve again but was used as a recruiting tool to get Negros to sign up for low-level jobs in the services.

He bitterly resented their treatment but said little, except to Rebecca.

Gilbert's death in 1909 hit the family very hard.

There was a large gathering of Prescott employees as well as family. Over the years, Gilbert had quietly helped many Negro families in the Oranges to buy homes, start businesses, and get an education.

He bequeathed a fund to Howard University for children of families in East Orange and surrounding towns.

James Prescott was curious as to the deposition of Gilbert's shares in the company but refrained from asking.

Over the next months, he found out Billie and Abraham shared equally.

He approached both about buying their shares, but both refused, more out of sentiment than any other reason.

Sabrina continued to manage the family money, increasingly irritating Billie.

In fact, the money was the only thing they ever fought over.

Jasmine was turning out to be a highly talented singer, but prospects for her in America were slim.

Increasingly frustrated by lack of opportunities to perform in America, she left for Paris on her seventeenth birthday to study there.

She never saw her mother or father again.

Before Sabrina died, she asked Abraham to manage Billie's money, but he refused. Surprisingly, her death sobered up Billie, and he became a much more conservative spender.

The two brothers agreed that the Prescott stock should go to Jasmine when they died.

Abraham died in the influenza epidemic of 1919–1920.

Billie followed in a few years, with his daughter still in Paris.

William Prescott Sr. 1903

Rebecca Prescott did not weep at her father's funeral. Her son, James Prescott Jr., stood by her side. On the other side, James looked at the coffin and said nothing. To his left stood William III, now a teenager, but tall and ramrod stiff. Gilbert and Eliza flanked him, and behind them in the First Episcopal Church were ranks of Prescott employees, business associates, and retainers.

Abraham was in the back with his brother and sisters. They stood quietly, only Gilbert knowing how much the man in the coffin had done for their family.

Also in the back was Beatty, looking at the assembled mourners and knowing more than he liked about many of them.

Since returning from Cuba, and after ten years of service with Theodore Roosevelt, who sent a telegram of condolences, he was now serving the Prescott enterprises and others, and was comfortably rich and happy. He had served William Sr. and now Gilbert and James.

Becky's daughter was six and left home with Mary Pat, who was now nanny to a second generation of Prescotts.

Like many others in the church, Becky wondered about the Colonel's will. No one except Gilbert and the family lawyers knew what it contained.

The funeral entourage left the church and wended its way to Ferndale Cemetery. It was a gloomy day for a funeral. Gray clouds and threatening rain cast a dark shadow over the line of carriages. There were even two or three automobiles in the procession, scaring some of the horses.

The reception in the house lasted past eight o'clock, with Becky and James retiring after nine. They had separate but adjoining bedrooms. The door was open as they undressed.

"It was a nice ceremony," he said.

"Yes, very nice. There were a lot of people."

"Too many."

"It was nice they all came, and the telegrams were very effusive."

"Some people that should have been here weren't, and I'm surprised at some that came."

"Funerals bring out the best and worst of people."

"All the Gilberts came."

"And why shouldn't they? The Prescotts have done a lot for them."

"They've done a lot for the Prescotts."

"Do you know what is in the will?"

"No, your father was quite close lipped about it, and old Jenkins hasn't said a word."

"When will the will be read?"

"We're thinking Tuesday, to let everything simmer down."

"What do you think William III will get?"

"Haven't the foggiest. Your father wanted to keep the company in the family's hands; that I do know."

"Well, have a good night."

"You too."

The door was shut and James lay back on the bed, his clothes half done. He thought of Angela and wondered what she was doing on this Thursday without him. He turned the light off and rolled over, not bothering to undress anymore.

Becky took time to brush her hair and hang up her clothes. She thought of going to young James or to her daughter but thought better of it.

"Mary Pat will have everything under control," she excused herself.

That following Tuesday, William Sr.'s last words to his family and staff were read.

In effect, Gilbert and James would control the company until 1910. Becky and William III each inherited 49 percent of the company in trust. The nephew would gain control of his inheritance at age twenty-five, while Becky's was in trust for her children, to be divided equally by them when she died.

To the surprise of everyone, Gilbert was left 2 percent of Prescotts, without any restrictions.

James was to continue as trustee as long as he was married to Becky but got nothing should they divorce at any time prior to the death of either.

Henry's will charged him with building the Commonwealth Club.

It was an immense task, and one he really didn't want.

But his debt to Henry made it a requirement that he successfully accomplished.

In going about the task, James later found out there were a list of men his father-in-law knew would want to participate in the new club. Strangely, he left Gilbert's name off the list.

"He did that on purpose," Gilbert said. "He didn't think the club could get off the ground if it had a Negro man as a charter member."

Becky thought the club was something her son might enjoy and appreciated her father's gesture.

Gilbert's ownership rankled James but he said nothing, not even to Angela.

In his heart, he hated William for giving Gilbert something denied him.

Over the years, he learned to accept the situation but never fully reconciled himself.

Gilbert had argued with the Colonel when the will was being drawn but realized it was a way of giving his family great financial security.

He told only his wife about their fortune and continued to live within his salary, which was considerable for a Negro in that day.

Only when he was near death did he reveal it to his children, and one already knew.

With the will read, Rebecca settled down to a middle age of comfort and pleasure.

Mary Pat took care of the children, and she was free to do the things she loved and with the man she most loved.

Her feelings for James were mixed. He was kind, considerate, and smart.

When they made love, it was of a gentle kind, but it did not excite her like Abraham did.

Early in her relationship with James, she had divined there was another woman.

At first she was angry, but then she realized it gave her an excuse to be with Abraham.

She also knew being with him had dangers.

It added to her excitement, because only in bed with him did she truly feel like a woman.

James and Becky shared a common grief when their daughter died of polio in 1900.

After their daughter's death, they decided not to have any more children.

It was something James agreed to reluctantly, but that Becky embraced.

The decision left her free to carry on her affair with Abraham.

James came to divide his love between his three sons, for he considered William III a son.

He also vowed to help Angela's son as well.

One gave him great joy for the rest of his life, one vexed him to the end of his days, and the third left him with a great void of sorrow.

As the year ended, James sat at his desk and reviewed the year and his life. He was now in charge of Prescotts and knew soon he would be losing Gilbert. The man had served the family and the company loyally for more than forty-five years. He moved slowly, and there was an ominous cough that persisted, despite what any doctor said or did. He had long come to suspect Rebecca had a lover. He had Angela, so he did not begrudge her the secret she had.

We all have our secrets, don't we? he said to himself, then thought of William Jr. and the fate that awaited him in the office next door.

If it were not for you, I would not be here, he thought.

He opened the drawer and took out a picture of Angela and his four-year-old son Joseph. He smiled at them.

With the Colonel gone, all the weight of Prescotts rested with him.

But I don't own a single share, it pained him to think.

That thought was immediately driven from his mind by the fact that his son would inherit half the company.

"Not too bad a legacy from a man who came to this country penniless."

He thought briefly of the stewardess on the White Star Line ship.

Anger welled up again when he remembered the pawnbroker who had sold his father's watch before he could reclaim it.

Of his mother and sister he thought nothing.

He turned to the present and was immediately consumed with what he needed to do next.

He summoned his closest associates and waited for them to arrive. It was time to talk about the future.

Prescotts was large, sprawling, profitable enterprise with more than two thousand employees all beholden to him.

The Colonel and I made a bargain and we both kept it, he said to himself.

When they were assembled, he turned to the men who now helped him run Prescotts—strangers compared to Gilbert—and said, "Prescotts will go on as before, but we will make it even more successful."

They nodded in agreement and left.

James turned to the window and wondered what the future would bring.

Whatever it was, he was ready.

Epilogue

With the deaths of Henry, William, and Gilbert, the founding generation passed from the scene, leaving a vast fortune and a thriving company in the hands of another generation.

Himself another immigrant, James Camaron Prescott was left in charge of that legacy, in trust for the next generation. The founding immigrant, Peter Prescott, did some things people did not like but nonetheless prospered, gaining riches but not respect.

His son, Henry, and his wife, Rebecca, expanded the company through hard work, shrewd business practices, and adherence to honesty.

Their son William built on this legacy and created an empire stretching to the Mississippi River.

His wife left this world heartbroken, and his only son died in sordid circumstances. His daughter kept a lifelong secret, but both offspring left behind sons who would go on to greatness.

Through their father, Sam, and his association with the Prescotts, the Gilberts prospered beyond the dreams of almost any black family in America of this era.

Many of the other people who were drawn into the Prescott family efforts also did well.

For those who tried to harm the family's interests, a bitter fate befell them.

America was changing as this generation died, and with these changes came new challenges for Prescotts.

What happened to the company and its leaders is gist for another chronicle.

For sales, editorial information, subsidiary rights information or a catalog, please write or phone or e-mail
iBooks
Manhanset House
Shelter Island Hts., New York 11965,
1-800-68-BRICK Tel: 212-427-7139

ibooksinc.com
email: bricktower@aol.com

www.Ingram.com

For sales in the UK and Europe please contact our distributor,
Gazelle Book Services
White Cross Mills
Lancaster, LA1 4XS,
UK Tel: (01524) 68765 Fax: (01524) 63232 email:
jacky@gazellebooks.co.uk